America's Best
LODGE RECIPES

Blueberry Crisp
with Walnut
Streusel Topping

Page 95

Pumpkin Pecan
Muffins

Page 26

Our Favorite Recipes
❦ *Hand Picked For You* ❦

Printed in the United States of America
by G&R Publishing Co.

Distributed By:

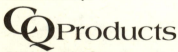

507 Industrial Street
Waverly, IA 50677

ISBN 1-56383-179-1
Item # 3803

Table of Contents

Cover Photo:
Point Au Roche Lodge
Plattsburgh, New York

Beverages, Sauces & Snacks

Wake Up Fruit Shake

Makes 2 servings

1 C. blueberries and
  raspberries with juice
1 container black cherry
  yogurt
1/2 C. ginger ale

1 C. vanilla ice cream
1 to 2 oz. wild raspberry
  liqueur
1 oz. triple sec

Place glasses in freezer 30 minutes prior to serving shakes. In a blender, combine berries with juice, black cherry yogurt, ginger ale, vanilla ice cream and liqueur. Blend until smooth and creamy or lightly lumpy, depending on preference. Immediately pour equal amounts of blended shake into frosted glasses. If desired, garnish with fresh mint, fresh flowers or strawberries.

Variation
Use any combination of fruits and yogurt in this shake. Use bananas sparingly, as the flavor will overpower all other ingredients.

The Lodge at Moosehead Lake
Greenville, Maine

Silver Bells Punch

1 (46 oz.) can
  unsweetened pineapple
  juice, chilled
2 C. Pina Colada drink
  mixer, chilled
1 (12 oz.) can frozen
  orange juice
  concentrate, thawed

1 liter club soda,
  chilled
1 liter lemon-lime soda,
  chilled
1 (10 oz.) pkg. frozen
  raspberries in syrup,
  drained

In a large punch bowl, combine pineapple juice, Pina Colada mixer, orange juice concentrate, club soda and lemon-lime soda. Mix until evenly blended. Before serving, stir in drained raspberries and serve chilled.

Rocky Mountain Lodge & Cabins
Cascade, Colorado

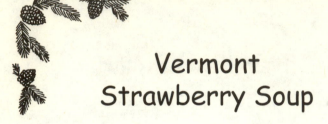

Vermont Strawberry Soup

3 to 4 C. frozen strawberries, partially thawed	2 to 3 T. sugar
	3/4 C. apple cider
	1/4 C. heavy cream

In a blender, combine strawberries, sugar and apple cider. Blend well until mixture is smooth. Add heavy cream and pulse until mixture is evenly pink. Be careful not to over mix or the cream may separate. Spoon into bowls. If desired, garnish with a sprig of fresh mint.

Variation
For a lower-fat version, use half n' half or low fat milk in place of heavy cream. May be served as a smoothie in a wine glass or goblet, garnished with a strawberry on the rim.

Moose Meadow Lodge
Waterbury, Vermont

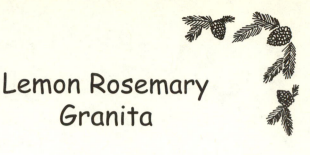

Lemon Rosemary Granita

Makes 6 servings

2 lemons
3 C. water
3/4 C. sugar

1/4 C. fresh chopped
rosemary, wrapped
in a cheesecloth bag

Zest the lemons and finely mince the zest. Squeeze juice from lemons to make about 1/2 cup. In a medium saucepan, bring water, sugar and minced lemon zest to a boil. Remove saucepan from heat and add rosemary bag, stirring carefully. Cover saucepan and let mixture cool to room temperature. Stir in lemon juice and remove rosemary bag. Pour syrup into a shallow dish or cake pan. Place pan in freezer until completely frozen, at least 5 hours or overnight. Chill an empty 2-quart container in the freezer. Using a metal spoon, scrape the surface of the frozen mixture and place in chilled container. Continue scraping frozen mixture until all is transferred to the chilled container. To serve, scoop granita into chilled bowls or glasses.

Snowbird Mountain Lodge
Robbinsville, North Carolina

Smoked Salmon Spread

Makes 12 servings

36 oz. cream cheese, softened
1/2 filet smoked salmon, de-boned
1/2 tsp. cayenne pepper
1 tsp. garlic powder

3 tsp. dried parsley flakes, divided
2 tsp. dried dillweed
2 to 4 T. grated Parmesan cheese

In a blender or food processor, combine cream cheese, smoked salmon, cayenne pepper, garlic powder, 2 teaspoons parsley flakes and dried dillweed. Blend until spread reaches desired consistency. Scoop into serving bowl and chill in refrigerator. Garnish with remaining 1 teaspoon parsley flakes and grated Parmesan cheese. Serve with fresh sliced baguette or crackers.

Sheep Mountain Lodge
Palmer, Alaska

Tartar Sauce

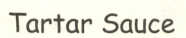

**1 C. Miracle Whip
salad dressing
1/4 C. finely chopped
onions**

**1/4 C. finely chopped
dill pickles**

In a small bowl, combine Miracle Whip salad dressing, finely chopped onions and finely chopped dill pickles. Mix until well blended. Place in a small serving bowl and, if desired, serve on the side with Northwest Angle Fried Fish (page 74) or other fish recipes.

*Prothero's Post Resort
Angle Inlet, Minnesota*

Cranberry Chutney

1 C. whole cranberries
1/2 C. brown sugar or
  1/4 C. honey
1 T. water
1/4 tsp. vanilla

1/4 tsp. grated orange
  peel
2 T. Cointreau liqueur
1/2 C. chopped walnuts,
  optional

In a medium pot, combine cranberries, brown sugar and water. Simmer mixture over medium heat for 10 minutes, until cranberries slightly pop open. Add vanilla, grated orange peel and liqueur. If desired, mix in chopped walnuts. Let mixture sit at room temperature for 15 minutes, until flavors blend. Store chutney in refrigerator. If desired, serve with "After the Fall" Pancakes (page 58), chicken or seafood.

Pond Mountain Lodge
Eureka Springs, Arkansas

Sweet Tomato Chutney

Makes 2 cups

1 head garlic, peeled and chopped	1 1/2 C. sugar
1 (2") piece fresh gingerroot, peeled and chopped	1 1/2 tsp. salt
	1/4 to 1/2 tsp. cayenne pepper
1 1/2 C. red wine vinegar, divided	2 T. golden raisins
2 lbs. fresh tomatoes, skinned	2 T. blanched slivered almonds

In a blender or food processor, puree chopped garlic, chopped gingerroot and 1/2 cup vinegar, until smooth. In a large pot, combine skinned tomatoes, remaining 1 cup vinegar, sugar, salt and cayenne pepper. Bring mixture to a boil. Add pureed mixture, reduce heat and let simmer for 2 to 3 hours, until thickened. Stir occasionally, and more frequently as chutney thickens. Mix in raisins and slivered almonds. Simmer, stirring often, for an additional 5 minutes. Remove from heat and let cool, until chutney reaches the consistency of honey. Store chutney in refrigerator.

A B&B at Llewellyn Lodge
Lexington, Virginia

Mushroom-Roquefort Sauce

1/4 lb. Roquefort cheese
1/2 C. butter
2 to 4 cloves garlic, minced
1 T. Worcestershire sauce
1/4 tsp. caraway seeds
1/2 C. chopped green onions, including green part
1/2 lb. sliced mushrooms

In a medium saucepan over low heat, combine Roquefort cheese, butter, minced garlic, Worcestershire sauce and caraway seeds. Stir until cheese and butter are melted. Add chopped green onions and sliced mushrooms. Continue heating for 2 to 3 minutes. If desired, serve over Trappers' Peak Tenderloin (page 61) or other meat.

Devils Tower Lodge
Devils Tower, Wyoming

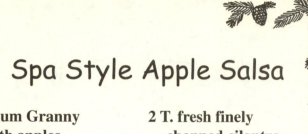

Spa Style Apple Salsa

3 medium Granny
   Smith apples
1 small to medium
   red onion
1 medium red bell
   pepper
1 jalapeno pepper,
   minced
1/3 C. dried currants

2 T. fresh finely
   chopped cilantro
2 tsp. grated orange peel
3/4 C. fresh orange juice
2 T. Dijon mustard
1 T. cumin
1/2 C. vegetable oil
1 T. dark sesame oil

Dice apples, red onion and red bell pepper into 1/4" pieces. In a large bowl, combine diced apples, diced red onions, diced red pepper, minced jalapeno pepper, dried currants, chopped cilantro and grated orange peel. In a blender or food processor, combine orange juice, Dijon mustard and cumin. Process until smooth and gradually add vegetable and sesame oil until thickened. Pour blended mixture over diced apples mixture and toss until evenly coated. Chill in refrigerator at least 2 to 4 hours before serving to allow flavors to blend. If desired, serve with tortilla chips or crackers.

Lodge at Sedona – A Luxury B&B Inn
Sedona, Arizona

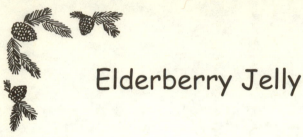

Elderberry Jelly

3 lbs. elderberries	1 box low-sugar pectin
1/2 C. lemon juice	5 C. sugar

Wash berries and pick over for quality. Place berries in a medium saucepan over low heat and cook until berries begin juicing. Let simmer for 15 minutes. Place a jelly bag or two layers of cheesecloth tightly over a separate saucepan. Pour berries and liquid over cloth and let drip overnight. In the morning, measure strained juice and add enough water to make 3 cups. Pour elderberry liquid into a saucepan over medium heat. Add lemon juice and pectin and bring to a boil. Add sugar and let boil for 1 additional minute. Mix well and pour jelly into sterilized jars and cap with canning lids. If desired, seal canning lids by placing jars in boiling water for 5 minutes.

Buffalo Run Lodge
Arbovale, West Virginia

Cranberry Relish

2 C. frozen cranberries   1/2 C. sugar
2 oranges, peeled, seeded
   and cut into pieces

In an old fashioned grinder, blender or food processor, combine frozen cranberries, oranges and sugar. Puree or grind until mixture reaches desired consistency. Serve on the side as a relish or, if desired, use in Cranberry Muffins recipe (page 23).

Ross' Teal Lake Lodge
Hayward, Wisconsin

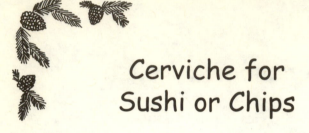

Cerviche for Sushi or Chips

1/2 C. lime juice
1 tsp. fresh grated
   gingerroot
1/4 C. soy sauce
Strips of salmon, from
   belly area of fish

1/2 C. tequila
1/2 C. brown sugar
1 T. coarse salt
1 red pepper, cut into
   strips

To make Sushi Cerviche, in a large bowl, combine lime juice, grated gingerroot and soy sauce. Add salmon strips and let marinate for 2 hours in the refrigerator. Remove salmon from bowl and cut into small, thin squares. Use in sushi or serve with various crackers. To make Cerviche for Chips, in a separate bowl, combine tequila, brown sugar, salt and red pepper strips. Mix well and add salmon strips. Let marinate for 2 hours in the refrigerator. Remove salmon from bowl and cut into small pieces. Serve on tortilla chips with a side of sour cream for dipping.

Nushagak Salmon Camp Lodge
Anchorage, Alaska

Brie & Crab Stuffed Mushrooms

Makes 18 stuffed mushrooms

18 large mushrooms, stems removed and reserved
2 T. butter, melted, divided
1 tsp. garlic salt
2 T. minced onion
1 tsp. Worcestershire sauce
4 oz. jumbo lump crabmeat
1 T. mayonnaise
3 oz. Brie cheese, cut into 18 small pieces

Preheat oven to 350°. Chop reserved mushroom stems and set aside. Place mushrooms caps upside-down on a lightly greased baking sheet. Brush caps with some of the melted butter and sprinkle with garlic salt. In a skillet, sauté chopped mushroom stems and minced onion in Worcestershire sauce and remaining melted butter. In a medium bowl, combine crabmeat and mayonnaise. Fill mushroom caps with sautéed onion mixture. Top each mushroom with crabmeat mixture and 1 piece of Brie cheese. Bake for 10 minutes, until mushrooms are tender and cheese is melted.

Rocky Mountain Lodge & Cabins
Cascade, Colorado

Paradise Popovers

Makes 12 servings

4 eggs	3 tsp. butter, divided
1 C. whole milk	Additional butter or
1 C. flour	jelly, optional
1/2 tsp. salt	

Preheat oven to 375°. Place a 12-cup mini muffin tin in hot oven for 3 minutes. In a large bowl, beat together eggs and whole milk. Stir in flour and salt, mixing just until evenly blended. Remove muffin tin from oven and place about 1/4 teaspoon butter in each cup. Return muffin tin to oven for an additional 1 to 2 minutes. Immediately pour batter in hot muffin tin to fill each cup 3/4 full. Quickly return muffin tin to oven. Bake for 30 to 35 minutes, making sure to keep oven door closed throughout cooking time. Serve immediately. If desired, spread with butter or jelly.

Pond Mountain Lodge
Eureka Springs, Arkansas

Marinated Cheese

1/2 C. olive oil
1/2 C. white wine
  vinegar
1 (2 oz.) jar diced
  pimentos, drained
3 T. fresh chopped
  parsley or cilantro
3 T. minced green onions
3 cloves garlic, minced
1 tsp. sugar

3/4 tsp. dried whole
  basil
1/2 tsp. salt
1/2 tsp. pepper
1 (8 oz.) block sharp
  Cheddar cheese, chilled
1 (8 oz.) pkg. cream cheese
  or Monterey Jack cheese
Fresh chopped parsley,
  optional

In a large jar with a lid, combine olive oil, vinegar, diced pimentos, chopped parsley, minced green onions, minced garlic, sugar, basil, salt and pepper. Cover jar tightly, shake vigorously and set aside. Cut blocks of Cheddar and cream cheese in half lengthwise. Cut halves crosswise into 1/4" thick slices. Arrange cheese slices, alternating, standing on edge, in a shallow baking dish. Pour mixture in jar over cheese slices. Cover and chill in refrigerator at least 8 hours. Remove cheese slices to a serving platter and spoon marinade from baking dish over slices. If desired, garnish with fresh chopped parsley. Serve with assorted crackers.

Mountain Top Lodge at Dahlonega
Dahlonega, Georgia

Deviled Egg Soufflé

Makes 4 servings

1 egg
1/2 C. milk, half n' half
   or heavy cream
2 T. flour
1/2 C. sherry

Pepper
Fresh chopped chives
4 T. shredded Swiss
   cheese, divided

Preheat oven to 400°. Grease 4 small ramekins and set aside. Once oven has heated, reduce heat to 350°. In a blender or food processor, combine egg, milk, flour and sherry at high speed for 1 minute. Pour equal amounts of blended mixture into each ramekin. Sprinkle pepper and chopped chives over mixture in each ramekin. Place ramekins on a baking sheet and bake for 25 to 30 minutes. Increase oven temperature to 400° for last 5 minutes of baking time. Eggs are done when golden brown and fluffing above ramekins. Remove from oven. If desired, turn out soufflé onto serving plates. Top each soufflé with 1 tablespoon shredded Swiss cheese.

The Lodge at Moosehead Lake
Greenville, Maine

Texas Tortilla Twisters

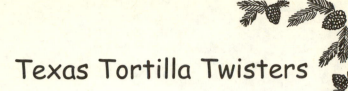

1 (8 oz.) pkg. cream
  cheese, softened
1 (8 oz.) container
  sour cream
5 green onions, chopped
1 (4 oz.) can chopped
  green chilies, drained

1/2 C. shredded sharp
  Cheddar cheese
2 T. chopped black olives
12 large flour tortillas
1 (8 oz.) jar picante sauce

In a blender or food processor, combine cream cheese, sour cream, chopped green onions, drained chilies, shredded sharp Cheddar cheese and chopped black olives. Process until smooth. Spread mixture evenly onto tortillas. Roll up tortillas. Wrap each tortilla in a damp paper towel. Place wrapped tortillas in an airtight plastic bag and refrigerate until ready to serve. To serve, remove paper towels from tortillas. Cut each rolled tortilla into 1" pinwheels. Serve twisters with toothpicks and a bowl of picante sauce for dipping.

Balsam Beach Resort & RV Park
Bemidji, Minnesota

Chili con Queso

1 yellow onion, chopped
2 Roma tomatoes, chopped
2 to 3 fresh jalapeno peppers, chopped
1 T. olive oil

1 lb. Velveeta cheese, cubed
1/2 C. shredded Cheddar cheese
1/2 C. shredded Monterey Jack cheese
Tortilla chips

In a medium skillet over medium heat, sauté chopped onions, chopped tomatoes and chopped jalapeno peppers in olive oil, until tender. Add Velveeta cheese cubes, shredded Cheddar cheese and shredded Monterey Jack cheese. Cook over low heat, until cheeses are melted. Serve with tortilla chips.

Cedar Rapids Lodge
Tenstrike, Minnesota

Breads
& Sides

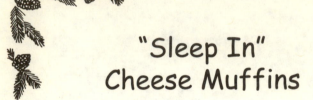

"Sleep In"
Cheese Muffins

1/2 C. self-rising flour
1/2 C. milk
1/4 C. mayonnaise

1 C. shredded cheese,
any kind, divided

Preheat oven to 450°. In a large bowl, combine flour, milk and mayonnaise. Mix in 3/4 cup shredded cheese. Spoon batter into greased muffin tins. Sprinkle tops of muffins with remaining 1/4 cup shredded cheese. Bake for 20 minutes.

Mountain Top Lodge at Dahlonega
Dahlonega, Georgia

Cranberry Muffins

Makes 3 dozen

4 1/2 C. flour, use
   1/2 whole wheat and
   1/2 white
2 1/2 C. sugar
1 1/2 tsp. baking soda
1/2 tsp. salt

2 eggs
1 1/2 C. buttermilk
1/2 C. oil
2 C. cranberry relish
  (page 13)

Preheat oven to 400°. In a large bowl, combine flour, sugar, baking soda and salt. Mix until well blended. Add eggs, buttermilk and oil. Blend gently, being careful not to overmix. About half of the flour should remain unmixed. Gently stir in cranberry relish. The batter should be white with red swirls. Pour batter into well greased medium muffin pans with 2 1/2" cups, filling cups 2/3 full with batter. Bake for 18 to 20 minutes, being careful not to overcook. If desired, batter can be baked into a loaf by pouring into a well greased loaf pan with waxed paper coating the bottom. Bake in 400° oven for 25 to 30 minutes, being careful not to overcook.

Note
Ross' Teal Lake Lodge uses cranberries from northern Wisconsin, where the flooded cranberry bogs glow with the rosey red of ripe cranberries in the September harvest.

Ross' Teal Lake Lodge
Hayward, Wisconsin

Peaches and Cream Muffins

Makes 1 dozen

2 C. flour
1 C. sugar
1 tsp. baking powder
1/2 tsp. baking soda
1 1/2 C. peeled and
   chopped fresh peaches

2 eggs
1 C. sour cream
1/2 C. vegetable oil
1/2 tsp. vanilla
1/2 tsp. almond extract

Preheat oven to 375°. In a large bowl, combine flour, sugar, baking powder and baking soda. Add chopped peaches and toss gently. In a medium bowl, combine eggs, sour cream, vegetable oil, vanilla and almond extract. Add eggs mixture to dry ingredients, mixing until just moistened. Pour batter into lightly greased or paper-lined muffin tins. Fill each cup 2/3 full with batter. Bake for 25 to 30 minutes or until a toothpick inserted in center comes out clean.

Lodge at Sedona – A Luxury B&B Inn
Sedona, Arizona

The Best Blueberry Muffins

Makes 2 dozen

3 1/4 C. flour
1 1/2 C. sugar
1 tsp. salt
4 tsp. baking powder
1 tsp. baking soda
Peel of 1 lemon, minced

1/2 C. chopped pecans
2 eggs
2 C. buttermilk
1/2 C. vegetable oil
2 C. frozen blueberries
Sugar for topping

Preheat oven to 375°. Line the cups of muffin tins with paper liners and spray liners with non-stick coating. Into a large bowl, sift flour, sugar, salt, baking powder and baking soda. Add minced lemon peel and chopped pecans. Set aside. In a separate bowl, whisk together eggs, buttermilk and vegetable oil until combined. Add egg mixture to flour mixture and stir just until the batter is combined. Gently fold in frozen blueberries, making sure to distribute as evenly as possible, being careful not to over mix. Spoon batter into prepared muffin pans. Sprinkle each muffin with a pinch of sugar. Bake for 23 to 25 minutes, until golden brown. Let muffins cool in pan for 10 minutes before removing to a wire rack.

A B&B at Llewellyn Lodge
Lexington, Virginia

Pumpkin Pecan Muffins

Makes 1 dozen

1 1/2 C. oats, divided
1 1/4 C. flour, divided
1 tsp. cinnamon
1/2 tsp. salt
1/2 tsp. nutmeg
1/2 tsp. baking soda
1/3 C. plus 3 T. chopped
   pecans, divided

1 C. canned pumpkin
1 C. brown sugar, divided
1/2 C. oil
1 egg
1/4 C. milk
1 tsp. vanilla
1/4 C. butter or
   margarine, softened

Preheat oven to 400°. Grease 12 muffin cups. In a large bowl, combine 1 1/4 cups oats, 1 cup flour, cinnamon, salt, nutmeg, baking soda and 1/3 cup chopped pecans. In a separate bowl, combine canned pumpkin, 3/4 cup brown sugar, oil, egg, milk and vanilla. Stir pumpkin mixture into dry ingredients. Pour batter into greased muffin cups. To make crumb topping, combine remaining 1/4 cup oats, remaining 1/4 cup flour and remaining 1/4 cup brown sugar. Using a pastry blender, cut butter into oat mixture. Mix in remaining 3 tablespoons chopped pecans. Sprinkle topping over muffins. Bake for 15 to 20 minutes.

Rocky Mountain Lodge & Cabins
Cascade, Colorado

Appalachian Trail
Bran Muffins

5 C. All Bran cereal,
   divided
2 C. boiling water
1 C. sugar
1 C. oil
2 C. molasses
1 C. buttermilk

4 eggs, beaten
5 C. self-rising flour
2 1/2 tsp. baking soda
1 tsp. salt
1 C. raisins, nuts or diced
   cooked apples, optional

Preheat oven to 400°. In a small bowl, combine 2 cups cereal and boiling water. Mix well and set aside to cool. In a large bowl, combine sugar, oil, molasses, buttermilk, beaten eggs and remaining 3 cups cereal, mixing well after each addition. In a separate bowl, combine flour, baking soda and salt. Mix well. Add flour mixture to buttermilk mixture and stir until well blended. Add cereal and boiling water mixture and blend well. If desired, mix in raisins, nuts or diced cooked apples. Fill the cups of greased muffin tins 3/4 full with batter. Bake for 15 to 20 minutes.

Mountain Top Lodge at Dahlonega
Dahlonega, Georgia

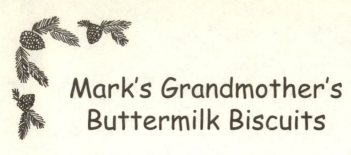

Mark's Grandmother's Buttermilk Biscuits

2 1/2 lbs. flour
1 T. salt
1 T. baking soda
1 T. cream of tartar
1/2 lb. Crisco shortening

4 C. buttermilk
Flour for dusting
1 C. sweet, unsalted
    butter, softened
3 T. butter, melted

Preheat oven to 425° to 450°. In a large bowl, combine flour, salt, baking soda and cream of tartar. Mix with a whisk until well combined. Work shortening into dry mixture using hands or a pastry cutter, until pea-sized crumbs form. Pour in buttermilk, using one hand to mix the dough and one hand to turn the bowl. Turn dough out onto a generously floured flat surface. Flour hands and dough. Pat dough into a 1" thick rectangle. Generously spread butter over dough to within 1" of the edges. Fold dough as follows: Take left side and fold to the middle, take right side and fold to the middle, fold top down to the middle and fold bottom edge up to the middle. Give the dough a 45° turn and pat dough again into a 1" thick rectangle, reflouring dough and surface as needed. Repeat folding process 2 more times, gently and quickly, being careful not to overwork dough. Cut dough using a 2" biscuit cutter and place rounds on a parchment-lined baking sheet, making sure biscuits touch each other. Bake for 10 to 15 minutes, until tops of biscuits are golden brown. Brush tops of biscuits with melted butter and serve immediately.

Snowbird Mountain Lodge
Robbinsville, North Carolina

Rosemary Biscuits

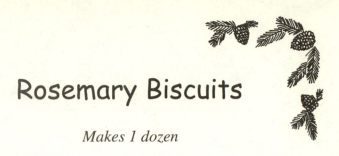

Makes 1 dozen

2 C. unbleached flour
1 1/2 T. baking powder
1 T. sugar
1/2 tsp. salt
1 T. fresh finely diced
    rosemary (or 1 1/2 tsp.
    dried rosemary)

1/2 C. unsalted butter,
    softened
1 egg, lightly beaten
3/4 C. buttermilk

Preheat oven to 425°. Into a large bowl, sift flour, baking powder, sugar and salt. Add rosemary and cut in butter until mixture is crumbly. In a small bowl, whisk together egg and buttermilk. Add to dry ingredients and stir until well moistened. Turn dough out onto a floured flat surface. Knead dough by hand for about 5 minutes. Roll dough into golf ball sized portions and place 1 1/2" apart on an ungreased baking sheet. Bake for 12 to 15 minutes, until lightly browned. Serve warm.

Mountain Home Lodge
Leavenworth, Washington

Banana Nut Bread

Makes 2 loaves

2 1/2 C. sugar
1 C. butter, melted
3 eggs
5 to 6 bananas, mashed
1 1/4 C. buttermilk

1 tsp. vanilla
3 C. flour
1 1/2 tsp. baking powder
1 1/2 tsp. baking soda
1 C. chopped nuts, optional

Preheat oven to 350°. In a large bowl, cream together sugar and melted butter. Stir in eggs, one at a time, and beat well. Mix in mashed bananas, buttermilk and vanilla. Add flour, baking powder and baking soda. If desired, mix in chopped nuts. Pour batter into two greased 5x9" loaf pans. Bake for 60 minutes.

Overleaf Lodge
Yachats, Oregon

Raisin Rye Bread

Makes 4 loaves

4 C. boiling water
2/3 C. molasses
1 T. salt
1/2 C. plus 1 tsp. sugar,
   divided

1/2 C. oil
3 C. medium rye flour
3 C. raisins
2 T. dry yeast
1/2 C. warm water

Preheat oven to 350°. In a large bowl, combine boiling water, molasses, salt, 1/2 cup sugar and oil. Let mixture cool to lukewarm. Add rye flour and mix until smooth. Stir in raisins. In a small bowl, dissolve yeast in warm water and add remaining 1 teaspoon sugar. Add yeast mixture to flour and molasses mixture. If needed, add more flour until dough is stiff. Knead dough until elastic. Let dough rise. Punch down dough and let rest 10 minutes. Shape dough into 4 large loaves and let rise. Place loaves into 4 greased 5x9" loaf pans. Bake for 45 minutes.

Boulder Lake Lodge
Pinedale, Wyoming

Jeanne's Cornbread Casserole

1 box Jiffy cornbread
  mix
1 can whole corn
  kernels, drained
1 can creamed corn
1/4 C. diced green chilies
1/4 to 1/2 C. salsa

1 egg
1/2 C. sour cream
1/4 to 1/2 C. butter,
  melted, optional
1 C. shredded cheese, any
  kind, divided

Preheat oven to 350°. In a large bowl, combine cornbread mix, drained corn, creamed corn, diced green chilies, salsa, egg, sour cream, melted butter and 1/2 cup shredded cheese. Pour into a lightly greased 9x13" baking dish or 2 smaller pans. Sprinkle remaining 1/2 cup shredded cheese over casserole. Bake for 30 to 40 minutes.

Sundance Bear Lodge
Mancos, Colorado

Pear, Walnut and Blue Cheese Flat Bread

1 T. dry active yeast
3 tsp. sugar, divided
1 1/2 C. warm water
3 C. flour
1/2 T. salt
1/2 C. chopped walnuts
2 T. olive oil
1 egg

2 to 4 T. cornmeal
2 C. pureed pears
3 oz. crumbled blue cheese
1/2 C. whole walnuts
1 C. shredded Monterey
   Jack cheese
1 T. fresh chopped
   rosemary

Preheat oven to 450°. In a medium bowl, combine yeast, 1 teaspoon sugar and warm water. Mix well and set aside. In a blender or food processor, combine flour, salt, chopped walnuts, olive oil, egg and remaining 2 teaspoons sugar. When a foam appears on top of yeast, add yeast to ingredients in blender or food processor and puree until evenly blended. Place dough in a well greased bowl and cover with plastic wrap. Let dough rise for 1 hour. Grease a full sheet pan and sprinkle with cornmeal. Press dough onto prepared pan. Spread pear puree over dough. Top pear puree with crumbled blue cheese, whole walnuts, shredded Monterey Jack cheese and chopped rosemary. Bake for 15 minutes, until cheeses are melted and slightly browned. To serve, cut bread into 1"x1" squares and place on serving platter. If desired, serve with herbed vinegar and garlic spread.

Lodge at Sedona – A Luxury B&B Inn
Sedona, Arizona

Pumpkin Chocolate Chip Bread

Makes 2 loaves

3 1/2 C. flour	4 eggs, beaten
2 tsp. baking soda	2/3 C. water
1 1/2 tsp. salt	1 C. vegetable oil
2 tsp. cinnamon	2 C. canned pumpkin
2 tsp. nutmeg	1 C. chocolate chips
3 C. sugar	1 C. chopped pecans

Preheat oven to 350°. Grease two 5x9" loaf pans and set aside. In a large mixing bowl, combine flour, baking soda, salt, cinnamon, nutmeg and sugar. Mix in beaten eggs, water, vegetable oil and canned pumpkin. Stir until well blended. Fold in chocolate chips and chopped pecans. Mix well and pour into prepared pans. Bake for 60 minutes.

Overleaf Lodge
Yachats, Oregon

Classy Cheese Grits Soufflé

2 T. butter
1 1/2 C. whole milk
1 1/2 C. water
1/2 tsp. salt
3/4 C. grits
1 C. shredded Cheddar
  cheese

2 T. granulated garlic
4 eggs, separated
Dash of white pepper
Dash of cayenne pepper

Preheat oven to 350°. In a glass soufflé dish, melt butter by placing dish in hot oven. Swirl dish until thoroughly coated with butter. In a medium saucepan over medium heat, heat whole milk, water and salt until almost boiling. Slowly stir in grits. Cook mixture for 5 minutes, stirring occasionally, over low heat. Stir in shredded Cheddar cheese, granulated garlic, lightly beaten egg yolks, white pepper and cayenne pepper. In a medium mixing bowl, beat egg whites at high speed until soft peaks form. Gently fold egg whites into grits mixture. Pour mixture into soufflé dish. Bake for 30 to 40 minutes, until lightly browned on top and edges.

Pond Mountain Lodge
Eureka Springs, Arkansas

Creamy Hash Browns

Makes 12 servings

1 (10 3/4 oz.) can cream
  of mushroom soup
1 (10 3/4 oz.) can cream
  of chicken soup
1 (8 oz.) container
  sour cream
1/2 C. milk
1/4 tsp. pepper

1 (30 oz.) bag frozen,
  shredded hash browns,
  partially thawed
8 medium green onions,
  sliced (about 1/2 C.)
1 C. shredded Cheddar
  or Colby Jack cheese

Preheat oven to 350°. Grease bottom and sides of a 9x13" baking dish or 12 small ramekins. In a large bowl, combine cream of mushroom soup, cream of chicken soup, sour cream, milk and pepper. Stir in hash browns and sliced green onions. Spoon mixture into baking dishes. Bake for 30 minutes. Sprinkle with shredded cheese. Bake an additional 15 to 20 minutes, until hash browns are golden brown and bubbly around edges.

Rocky Mountain Lodge & Cabins
Cascade, Colorado

Davey Crockett Potatoes

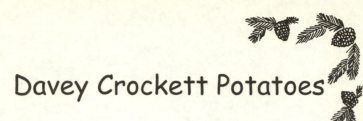

4 lbs. new red potatoes,
   sliced into thin rounds
2 small bags baby
   carrots, sliced
   lengthwise

2 bunches green onions,
   chopped
2 T. seasoning salt
1 T. pepper
1/2 lb. butter

Preheat oven to 350°. In a large roasting pan, combine sliced red potatoes, sliced carrots, chopped green onions, seasoning salt, pepper and butter. Mix until vegetables are evenly coated. Bake for 1 hour, until potatoes are tender. If desired, wrap potatoes in individual foil packets and heat over grill.

Pike Point Resort & Lodge
Tenstrike, Minnesota

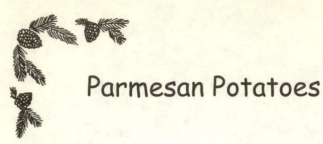

Parmesan Potatoes

4 large potatoes,
divided

2 T. lemon pepper,
divided

2 T. garlic powder,
divided

2 T. Italian seasoning,
divided

1/4 C. grated Parmesan
cheese, divided

3 T. olive oil

Preheat oven to 350°. Wash potatoes and cut into 1/2" cubes. Layer half of the potatoes in a greased 9x13" baking dish. Sprinkle 1 tablespoon lemon pepper, 1 tablespoon garlic powder, 1 tablespoon Italian seasoning and 1/8 cup grated Parmesan cheese over potatoes. Repeat layers with remaining half of potatoes, remaining 1 tablespoon lemon pepper, remaining 1 tablespoon garlic powder, remaining 1 tablespoon Italian seasoning and remaining 1/8 cup grated Parmesan cheese. Drizzle olive oil over potatoes. Cover baking dish with aluminum foil and bake for 1 hour.

Buffalo Run Lodge
Arbovale, West Virginia

Easy Oven Potatoes

2 lb. frozen hash
  brown potatoes,
  thawed
1 can cream of
  mushroom soup
1 1/2 C. butter,
  melted, divided

10 oz. shredded
  Cheddar cheese
2 C. sour cream
1 tsp. salt
1/4 tsp. pepper
2 C. crushed corn flakes

Preheat oven to 350°. In a large bowl, combine hash brown potatoes, cream of mushroom soup, 1 cup melted butter, shredded Cheddar cheese, sour cream, salt and pepper. Spread hash brown mixture evenly into a lightly greased 9x13" baking dish. In a separate bowl, combine crushed corn flakes and remaining 1/2 cup melted butter. Mix until evenly coated. Sprinkle corn flakes mixture over potatoes in pan. Bake for 45 minutes.

Balsam Beach Resort & RV Park
Bemidji, Minnesota

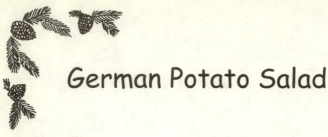

German Potato Salad

6 lbs. potatoes	1 1/4 C. vinegar
Seasoning salt	3/4 C. sugar
1 lb. bacon	1/2 pkg. Good Seasons
2 bunches green	salad dressing mix
onions, chopped	1 1/2 C. water
2 to 3 T. flour	Paprika

Fill a large pot with water and boil potatoes with skins on. Peel potatoes when warm. Layer potatoes in a large casserole dish and sprinkle with seasoning salt. Preheat oven to 350°. In a large skillet over medium high heat, fry bacon and pour off half of the grease. Crumble bacon and return to skillet. Add chopped green onions and sauté slightly. Add flour, vinegar, sugar, salad dressing mix and water. Pour mixture over potatoes in casserole dish. Sprinkle with paprika and bake, covered, for 45 minutes. Uncover casserole dish and bake an additional 15 minutes. Serve warm.

Boyd Lodge
Crosslake, Minnesota

Strawberry Spinach Salad

1 bunch fresh spinach,
 washed and torn
2 T. sesame seeds,
 toasted*
2 C. fresh strawberries,
 halved
1/4 C. safflower oil

2 T. salad vinegar
2 T. sugar
2 T. minced onions
1/2 tsp. salt
Pinch of pepper
Dash of Tabasco sauce

In a large glass bowl, combine torn spinach, toasted sesame seeds and strawberries. In a medium bowl, whisk together safflower oil, salad vinegar, sugar, minced onions, salt, pepper and Tabasco sauce. Just before serving, toss salad dressing with spinach mixture until evenly coated. Serve immediately.

* To toast, place sesame seeds in a single layer on a baking sheet. Bake at 350° for approximately 10 minutes or until sesame seeds are golden brown.

Pike Point Resort & Lodge
Tenstrike, Minnesota

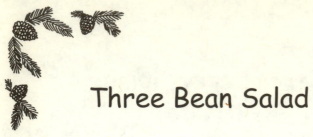

Three Bean Salad

Makes 10 to 12 servings

1 can green beans, drained	1 C. sliced celery
1 can wax beans, drained	1/2 C. chopped onions
1 can kidney beans, drained	1 jar button mushrooms
1 small green pepper, chopped	1/2 C. vegetable oil
	3/4 C. sugar
	2/3 C. vinegar
	1/2 tsp. salt
	1/2 tsp. pepper

In a large bowl, combine drained green beans, drained wax beans, drained kidney beans, chopped green peppers, sliced celery, chopped onions and button mushrooms. In a medium bowl, combine vegetable oil, sugar, vinegar, salt and pepper. Pour mixture over vegetables and marinate overnight in refrigerator before serving.

Boyd Lodge
Crosslake, Minnesota

Fall Vegetables

2 T. olive oil
2 T. unsalted butter
1 sweet potato, peeled
  and carved with a
  melon ball knife
1 celery root, peeled
  and cut into 1" pieces
8 spring onions, white
  part only

2 parsnips, peeled and
  cut into 1" pieces
3 strips blanched orange
  zest
2 T. maple syrup
1 T. fresh lemon juice
1 C. chicken broth, divided
Salt and pepper

In a large saucepan over medium heat, combine olive oil and butter until melted. Add sweet potatoes, celery root, spring onions, parsnips and orange zest. Sauté vegetables for 5 minutes, stirring frequently. Add maple syrup, lemon juice and 1/2 cup chicken broth. Heat until liquid is reduced to a glaze. Add remaining 1/2 cup chicken broth, cooking until heated throughout. Season with salt and pepper.

The Lodge and Spa at Cordillera
Edwards, Colorado

Asian Slaw

2/3 C. rice wine vinegar
3 T. sugar
1 tsp. honey
1 tsp. soy sauce
2 T. fresh chopped
   cilantro
1 T. sesame seeds,
   toasted*

1 head Napa cabbage,
   shredded
2 Asian pears, peeled
   and diced
1/2 C. shredded carrots
1/4 C. chopped green
   onions
1/4 C. diced red bell pepper

In a large bowl, combine rice wine vinegar, sugar, honey, soy sauce, chopped cilantro and sesame seeds. In a large salad bowl, combine shredded cabbage, diced pears, shredded carrots, chopped green onions and diced red bell pepper. Pour rice wine vinegar mixture over cabbage mixture and toss until evenly coated. Let stand for 20 minutes before serving. If desired, garnish slaw with additional chopped green onions and toasted sesame seeds. Slaw is excellent served with grilled meats and fish.

* To toast, place sesame seeds in a single layer on a baking sheet. Bake at 350° for approximately 10 minutes or until sesame seeds are golden brown.

Lodge at Sedona – A Luxury B&B Inn
Sedona, Arizona

Broccoli Slaw

2 pkgs. broccoli cole
   slaw
8 oz. cole slaw dressing
1 C. craisins

1 clove garlic, minced
1 T. finely chopped
   sweet onions
1 C. cashews

In a large bowl, combine broccoli cole slaw, cole slaw dressing, craisins, minced garlic and finely chopped sweet onions. Mix until evenly blended. Chill mixture in refrigerator. Before serving, fold in cashews. Serve cold.

Boyd Lodge
Crosslake, Minnesota

Norwegian Rice

1/2 gallon whole milk	1 tsp. vanilla
1 C. white rice	1 egg
3/4 C. sugar	

In a medium saucepan, combine whole milk and white rice. Cook slowly over low heat for 1 hour, stirring often, until rice is soft. In a medium bowl, combine sugar, vanilla and egg. Mix well and stir into cooked rice. Serve on the side as a warm sweet custard.

Cedar Rapids Lodge
Tenstrike, Minnesota

Great Granola

1 C. butter
1 C. honey
12 C. old fashioned oats
1 (7 oz.) pkg. shredded
   coconut
4 C. unsalted sunflower
   seeds

2 C. chopped walnuts
   or almonds
5 tsp. cinnamon
1 C. wheat germ, optional
1 C. raisins
1 C. dried cranberries

Preheat oven to 350°. In a small saucepan over medium heat, melt butter and honey together. In a large bowl, combine oats, shredded coconut, sunflower seeds, chopped nuts and cinnamon. Pour melted butter mixture over dry ingredients and stir until evenly coated. Pour granola in an even layer into a greased 9x13" baking dish. Bake for 15 minutes, stirring several times. If desired, stir in wheat germ. Bake for an additional 10 minutes, until lightly browned. Remove from oven and stir in raisins and cranberries. Let cool completely before storing in an airtight container.

Overleaf Lodge
Yachats, Oregon

Baked Oatmeal

6 C. quick oats	4 tsp. baking powder
1 C. brown sugar	1 C. salad oil
1 C. sugar	2 C. milk
2 tsp. salt	4 eggs, beaten

Preheat oven to 350°. In a large bowl, combine oats, brown sugar, sugar, salt and baking powder until well blended. Stir in salad oil, milk and beaten eggs. Mix until well blended. Pour mixture into a greased 9x13" baking dish. Bake for 30 minutes, until oatmeal is set. Middle of oatmeal may be slightly unset. Serve warm.

Boulder Lake Lodge
Pinedale, Wyoming

Main Dishes & Soups

Wolf Lodge Creek Breakfast MexiGrands

Makes 6 servings

1/2 lb. pork sausage
1/4 C. chopped scallions
1 (1 1/4 oz.) pkg. taco
    seasoning mix
6 eggs, beaten
1/4 C. picante sauce

1 tsp. salt
1 1/2 C. shredded Monterey
    Jack cheese, divided
1 pkg. 8 refrigerated
    jumbo biscuits, divided

Preheat oven to 375°. In a medium skillet over medium heat, sauté pork sausage, scallions and taco seasoning. Drain mixture and set aside. In a large skillet over medium heat, cook beaten eggs. When eggs are almost cooked through, add sausage mixture and picante sauce to skillet, stirring well. Stir in salt and 1 cup shredded Monterey Jack cheese and set aside. Roll out 6 biscuits, each into an approximately 5 1/2" circle. Mold biscuits into greased jumbo muffin tins. Add 1/2 cup of the egg mixture to each cup. Top with remaining 1/2 cup shredded Monterey Jack cheese. Roll out remaining 2 biscuits and cut into six 3" rounds. Place rounds on top of filling in muffin cups. Bake for 12 minutes. If desired, serve with salsa on the side.

Wolf Lodge Creek B&B
Coeur d'Alene, Idaho

Buffalo Run
Breakfast Strata

Makes 6 to 8 servings

Seasoned croutons
1/2 lb. shredded
   Cheddar cheese,
   divided
12 slices cooked bacon,
   sausage or ham,
   divided
1/2 C. sliced fresh
   mushrooms, divided

1/2 C. sliced sun-dried
   tomatoes, divided
8 eggs, beaten
3 C. milk
1 tsp. mustard
Salt and pepper to taste

Layer seasoned croutons over the bottom of a greased 9x13" baking dish. Cover croutons with half of the shredded Cheddar cheese, half of the cooked meat, half of the mushrooms and half of the sun-dried tomatoes. Repeat layers of shredded Cheddar cheese, cooked meat, mushrooms and sun-dried tomatoes. In a large bowl, beat together eggs, milk, mustard, salt and pepper. Pour egg mixture over ingredients in pan. Cover and refrigerate overnight. Preheat oven to 325°. Bake for 50 to 60 minutes or until a toothpick inserted in center comes out clean. Let stand for 5 to 10 minutes before serving.

Buffalo Run Lodge
Arbovale, West Virginia

51

Aunt Mary Ann's
Apple French Toast

1/2 C. butter
1 C. brown sugar
2 T. syrup
1 tsp. cinnamon
1/8 tsp. ground cloves
4 to 6 Granny Smith
   apples, peeled and
   sliced

1 C. milk
3 eggs
1 tsp. vanilla
1 loaf French bread,
   cut into 1" slices

Preheat oven to 350°. In a medium saucepan over medium heat, combine butter, brown sugar, syrup, cinnamon and ground cloves, until melted. Spread melted mixture over the bottom of a 9x13" baking dish. Lay peeled and sliced apples over mixture in pan. In a medium bowl, combine milk, eggs and vanilla. Dip French bread slices into milk mixture and lay bread slices over apples in pan. Pour any remaining milk mixture over bread slices in pan. Bake for 35 to 45 minutes, until golden brown.

Liars' Lodge B&B
Buena Vista, Colorado

Peach Stuffed French Toast

10 to 12 slices white
   bread, crusts
   removed
4 eggs, divided
2 C. half n' half

3/4 C. sugar, divided
2 tsp. vanilla, divided
8 oz. cream cheese, softened
1 (16 oz.) can sliced peaches,
   drained

Preheat oven to 350°. Arrange half of the bread slices in the bottom of a greased 7x11" baking dish. In a medium bowl, beat together 3 eggs, half n' half, 1/2 cup sugar and 1 teaspoon vanilla. Pour half of the mixture over bread in baking dish. In a separate bowl, combine cream cheese, remaining 1 egg, remaining 1/4 cup sugar and remaining 1 teaspoon vanilla. Spread cream cheese mixture over bread in baking dish. Place drained peaches over cream cheese mixture in baking dish. Top with remaining bread slices and remaining half n' half mixture. Cover and bake for 30 minutes. Uncover and bake an additional 30 minutes, until puffy and golden brown.

Wolf Lodge Creek B&B
Coeur d'Alene, Idaho

Egg Wraps

1 2/3 C. beaten eggs
1/3 C. heavy whipping
cream
3 T. sun-dried tomato
pesto

2 tomato tortillas
4 T. shredded Cheddar
cheese, divided

Preheat oven to 350°. In a thoroughly greased small square plastic container, place beaten eggs, heavy cream and sun-dried tomato pesto. Microwave for 6 minutes. Remove from microwave and cut mixture into 5 long strips. Lay tortillas flat and sprinkle 1 tablespoon shredded Cheddar cheese in a line in the middle of each tortilla. Place 2 1/2 strips egg mixture over cheese on each tortilla and cover with remaining 2 tablespoons shredded Cheddar cheese. Tightly wrap tortillas and cut into 1" sections. Place wraps on a parchment lined baking sheet. Bake for 5 minutes, until cheese is melted.

Overleaf Lodge
Yachats, Oregon

Breakfast Frittata

Makes 8 servings

1 T. vegetable oil
2 C. frozen shredded
   potatoes
4 large eggs
1/2 C. milk
1/4 tsp. salt

1/4 C. chopped tomatoes
1/4 C. sliced green onions
1/2 C. shredded Cheddar
   cheese
1/2 C. shredded mozzarella
   cheese

In a large oven-safe skillet, heat oil. Add shredded potatoes and cook over low medium heat. In a large bowl, beat together eggs, milk and salt. Pour egg mixture over potatoes in skillet. Sprinkle chopped tomatoes and sliced green onions over top. Cover and cook over low heat for 5 to 7 minutes. Uncover and sprinkle with shredded Cheddar and shredded mozzarella cheese. Continue cooking until center of frittata is set. Place frittata under broiler until cheese is melted and lightly browned. Let frittata cool on a wire rack for 10 minutes before cutting into wedges.

Mountain Top Lodge at Dahlonega
Dahlonega, Georgia

Oven Omelet

18 eggs　　　　　　　1 tsp. salt
1 C. sour cream　　　1/4 C. chopped green
1 C. milk　　　　　　　onions

Preheat oven to 350°. In a large bowl, combine eggs, sour cream, milk and salt. Mix well and pour mixture into a greased 9x13" baking dish. Sprinkle chopped green onions over egg mixture in pan. Bake for 40 to 45 minutes.

Liars' Lodge B&B
Buena Vista, Colorado

Baked Ham & Cheese Omelet

Makes 8 servings

12 eggs
1/2 C. evaporated milk
1/4 to 1/2 tsp. salt
Pepper to taste
1/2 C. chopped cooked
   ham

3/4 C. shredded Cheddar
   cheese, divided
1/4 C. finely chopped
   yellow onions
2 T. butter
2 T. fresh chopped parsley

Preheat oven to 350°. In a large bowl, beat eggs and evaporated milk until well blended. Add salt, pepper, chopped ham and 1/2 cup shredded Cheddar cheese, stirring until well coated. In a medium oven-safe skillet, sauté chopped yellow onions in butter for 2 to 3 minutes. Add egg mixture to skillet and place in oven. Using a long spatula, lift egg mixture from sides and bottom of skillet every 10 minutes, until eggs are fully cooked. Sprinkle with remaining 1/4 cup shredded Cheddar cheese and fresh chopped parsley.

Boulder Lake Lodge
Pinedale, Wyoming

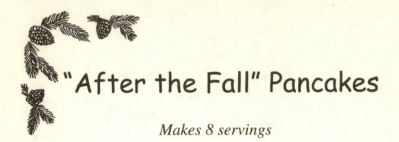

"After the Fall" Pancakes

Makes 8 servings

1 1/2 C. shredded ricotta cheese	1 tsp. nutmeg
1 C. flour	2 tsp. cinnamon
1/2 C. whole wheat flour	Pinch of salt
3 T. brown sugar	7 or 8 eggs, well beaten
1/4 C. slivered almonds	Yogurt, sour cream, syrup
2 C. finely diced Rome, McIntosh or Jonathon apples	or Cranberry Chutney (page 8) for topping, optional

In a large bowl, combine shredded ricotta cheese, flour, whole wheat flour, brown sugar, slivered almonds and finely diced apples. Add nutmeg, cinnamon and salt. Add beaten eggs, being careful not to overmix. Mixture should be lumpy. In a medium hot skillet, heat butter or light oil. Fry 1/8 of the batter in hot skillet, flipping to cook both sides, until golden brown. Repeat with remaining batter. If desired, serve pancakes with yogurt, sour cream, syrup or Cranberry Chutney (page 8).

Pond Mountain Lodge
Eureka Springs, Arkansas

Mile High Quiche

Makes 6 to 8 servings

1 (9") pastry pie crust
7 eggs, divided
1/2 lb. sliced bacon
2 green onions, chopped,
    optional
3 C. shredded Swiss
    cheese

1 1/4 tsp. salt
1/8 tsp. nutmeg
1/8 tsp. pepper
Pinch of cayenne pepper
3 C. light cream

Preheat oven to 375°. Fit pastry pie crust into a greased 9" springform pan. Separate 1 egg, reserving yolk, and brush egg white onto pie crust. In a large sauté pan, fry bacon until crispy. Drain bacon of fat and crumble bacon onto bottom of pie crust. If desired, sprinkle chopped green onions over bacon. Sprinkle shredded Swiss cheese over bacon and onions. In a large bowl, combine remaining 6 eggs, reserved egg yolk, salt, nutmeg, pepper, cayenne pepper and light cream. Beat until well combined, but not frothy. Slowly pour mixture over ingredients in pie crust. Bake for 50 to 55 minutes, until golden brown and puffy. Remove to a wire rack and let cool for 15 minutes. Loosen edge of quiche with a sharp knife and gently remove sides of springform pan. Leave bottom of pan in place and transfer quiche to a serving plate.

A B&B at Llewellyn Lodge
Lexington, Virginia

Taco Salad

1 large head of lettuce
2 tomatoes, chopped
1 can red beans, drained
1 lb. shredded pizza-
   flavored cheese

1 large bottle Catalina or
   western dressing
1 large bag corn chips

Tear head of lettuce into little pieces. In a large bowl, combine lettuce pieces, chopped tomatoes, drained red beans, shredded cheese, dressing and corn chips. Mix until evenly incorporated. Serve immediately.

Balsam Beach Resort & RV Park
Bemidji, Minnesota

Trappers' Peak Tenderloin

Makes 6 to 8 servings

1 (4 lb.) whole beef tenderloin	3/4 C. Worcestershire sauce
2 to 4 cloves garlic, minced	1 1/2 C. soy sauce
4 to 6 T. coarsely ground black pepper	1 1/3 C. beef broth
	Mushroom-Roquefort Sauce (page 10), optional

Thoroughly wash tenderloin and pat dry. Rub tenderloin with minced garlic and press black pepper onto sides. In a large baking dish, combine Worcestershire sauce and soy sauce. Marinate beef in baking dish for 2 to 3 hours at room temperature. Preheat oven to 500°. Drain baking dish and discard marinade. Pour broth around beef. Transfer to oven and immediately reduce heat to 350°. For rare meat, cook for 18 minutes per pound. For medium rare, cook for 20 minutes per pound or until internal temperature reaches 135° to 140°. Slice tenderloin and, if desired, serve with Mushroom-Roquefort Sauce (page 10).

Note
The US FDA recommends marinating foods in the refrigerator. They also recommend cooking steaks to at least 145°F.

Devils Tower Lodge
Devils Tower, Wyoming

Steak Italiano

Makes 4 servings

3 cloves garlic	1/2 C. marinara sauce,
1 T. dried rosemary	divided
1 tsp. dried oregano	1/2 C. shredded Romano
1 tsp. salt	cheese, divided
2 tsp. peppercorns	Fresh chopped parsley
4 (12 oz.) strip steaks	for garnish
1/2 C. beef broth, divided	

Preheat grill. Using a mortar and pestle, mash together garlic, rosemary, oregano, salt and peppercorns. Coat each steak with a generous amount of garlic mixture. Charbroil or grill steaks to rare or medium rare. While grilling, place beef broth and marinara sauce in separate, microwave-safe bowls. Heat in microwave for 1 to 2 minutes. When steaks are done, top each steak with 2 tablespoons shredded Romano cheese. Place steaks under broiler until cheese is melted and lightly browned. Place steaks on serving plates and top each steak with 2 tablespoons broth and 2 tablespoons marinara sauce. Sprinkle steaks with fresh chopped parsley. Steak is excellent served with pasta and hot garlic bread.

Note
The US FDA recommends cooking steaks to at least 145°F.

Canyon Crest Lodge
Pagosa Springs, Colorado

Crock Pot Chicken

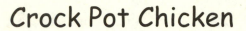

**6 to 8 boneless skinless
  chicken breast halves
1 pkg. dry onion soup
  mix**

**1 jar apricot preserves
1 bottle low-fat Italian
  dressing**

In a large crock pot, combine chicken breast halves, onion soup mix, apricot preserves and Italian dressing. Cook on low for 4 hours. If desired, serve over rice or noodles.

Variation
Can substitute 1 can whole cranberries for apricot preserves.

Pike Point Resort & Lodge
Tenstrike, Minnesota

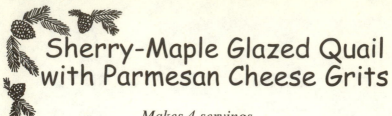

Sherry-Maple Glazed Quail with Parmesan Cheese Grits

Makes 4 servings

Zest of 1 lemon, divided	4 C. light chicken broth
1 tsp. fresh chopped thyme	1 C. grits
1 tsp. fresh chopped garlic	1/2 C. roasted garlic*
1/2 C. vegetable oil	1/2 C. grated Parmesan
1 T. balsamic vinegar	cheese
4 quail	1 T. fresh chopped herbs
1/2 C. sherry vinegar	(chervil, thyme, rosemary)
1/2 C. maple syrup	Salt and pepper

In a medium bowl, combine 1/2 of the lemon zest, chopped thyme, chopped garlic, vegetable oil and balsamic vinegar. Pour mixture over quail in a 9x13" baking dish and marinate in refrigerator for 4 hours. Grill quail over charcoal for 3 to 5 minutes on each side, until medium well. To make Sherry-Maple glaze, in a small pan over low medium heat, combine sherry vinegar and maple syrup. Reduce to a syrupy consistency and keep warm until grits are cooked. To prepare Parmesan Cheese Grits, in a medium pot, bring chicken broth to a boil. Add remaining 1/2 of the lemon zest, grits and roasted garlic. Cook over low heat for 10 to 12 minutes, until thickened. Add grated Parmesan cheese and chopped herbs. Season with salt and pepper. Divide hot grits evenly onto 4 warmed plates. Place 1 grilled quail on each plate and drizzle each with Sherry-Maple glaze.

* To make roasted garlic, preheat oven to 350°. In a pie pan, place 4 heads peeled garlic and 2 tablespoons olive oil. Sprinkle with salt and white pepper to taste. Bake until garlic is lightly browned. Transfer to a blender or food processor and blend until smooth.

Rough Creek Lodge
Glen Rose, Texas

Roasted Garlic
Tenderloin Medallions with
Mushroom Cognac Sauce

Makes 4 servings

2 T. extra-virgin olive oil	1 T. au jus base
1 lb. sliced mushrooms	1 tsp. fresh chopped basil
1 T. fresh chopped garlic	1 to 2 tsp. cornstarch
1 C. cognac	4 (8 oz.) tenderloin filets
1 C. water	2 tsp. roasted garlic*

Preheat oven to 350°. To make Mushroom Cognac sauce, in a large skillet over medium heat, heat olive oil. Sauté mushrooms and chopped garlic until tender. Add cognac, cooking until mixture is reduced by half. Add water, au jus base and chopped basil. Bring mixture to just boiling. In a small bowl, combine cornstarch and a little water. Thicken garlic mixture with cornstarch mixture. Mix and set aside. Cut a small slit in each tenderloin filet and insert 1/2 teaspoon roasted garlic in each slit. Roast tenderloins in heated oven and cook to desired doneness. Remove from oven and transfer tenderloins to serving plate. Cover with sauce and serve.

* To make roasted garlic, preheat oven to 350°. In a pie pan, place 2 heads peeled garlic and 2 tablespoons olive oil. Sprinkle with salt and white pepper to taste. Bake until garlic is lightly browned. Transfer to a blender or food processor and blend until smooth.

St. Germain Lodge
St. Germain, Wisconsin

Mark's Chicken 'N Dumplings

1 (2 1/2 to 3 lbs.) whole chicken, rinsed, gizzards removed
4 carrots, peeled, cut into 1/2" pieces, divided
2 stalks celery, cut into 1/2" pieces
2 onions, peeled and diced, divided
5 whole peppercorns
1 bay leaf
2 sprigs fresh parsley (or 1 tsp. dried parsley flakes)
4 sprigs fresh thyme (or 1 tsp. dried thyme)
2 sprigs fresh sage (or 1 tsp. dried sage)
6 T. butter
6 T. flour
2 parsnips, peeled and diced
8 oz. white button mushrooms, quartered
1 C. dry sherry
2 C. heavy cream
1/4 C. fresh chopped parsley
1/4 C. fresh chopped sage
Salt and pepper to taste
1 recipe buttermilk biscuits (page 28)

In a large pot, combine chicken, 1/2 the carrots, celery, 1/2 the onions, peppercorns, bay leaf, parsley, thyme and sage sprigs. Cover chicken completely with water and bring to a slow boil. Reduce heat and let simmer for 1 1/2 hours. Remove from heat and place chicken on a plate to cool. Strain broth, reserving liquid. When cooled, skin the chicken and remove bones. In a separate pot, melt butter over low medium heat and whisk in flour. Cook for 3 to 4 minutes, until light brown. Dice remaining 1/2 carrots and add to flour mixture. Stir in remaining 1/2 onions, parsnips and mushrooms and cook until vegetables soften. Slowly stir in sherry and reserved liquid and bring to a boil. Reduce heat and let simmer for 25 minutes, stirring often. Fold in heavy cream, chicken, chopped parsley, chopped sage, salt and pepper. Preheat oven to 450°. Pour chicken mixture into 1 or 2 large greased casserole dishes. Keep mixture warm while preparing biscuits. Prepare biscuits according to recipe and cut with a 1 1/2" biscuit cutter. Place biscuits over chicken, making sure to cover entire casserole. Bake for 18 to 20 minutes, until biscuits are golden brown.

Snowbird Mountain Lodge
Robbinsville, North Carolina

Scallopini

4 thin steaks or tender
   pieces of elk or deer
Salt
Flour
2 T. butter
1 C. beef or chicken
   broth

1/2 C. white wine
2 T. lemon juice
White pepper
1/4 C. capers
2 T. fresh chopped
   parsley, divided
Lemon wedges

Pound meat to 1/8" thickness. Sprinkle with salt and cover in flour. In a large frying pan, melt butter over medium high heat. Add meat and sauté quickly, until light brown. Set meat aside and keep warm in oven. Add broth, white wine and lemon juice to frying pan. Boil mixture until liquid reduces by 1/4. Add salt and white pepper to taste. Stir in capers and 1 tablespoon chopped parsley. Place meat on serving plate and pour sauce over meat. Garnish with remaining 1 tablespoon chopped parsley and lemon wedges. If desired, serve with rice or pasta of choice.

Canyon Crest Lodge
Pagosa Springs, Colorado

Sweet-and-Sour
Meat Loaf

Makes 6 servings

1 1/2 lbs. ground beef	1 (15 oz.) can tomato
1 C. dry bread crumbs	sauce, divided
1 tsp. salt	2 T. brown sugar
1/4 tsp. pepper	2 T. vinegar
2 eggs	1/2 C. sugar
1 tsp. minced onion	2 tsp. mustard

Preheat oven to 350°. In a large mixing bowl, combine ground beef, bread crumbs, salt, pepper and eggs. Add minced onion and half of the tomato sauce. Form meat mixture into a loaf and place in a 5x9" loaf pan. Bake for 50 minutes. In a saucepan over medium heat, bring remaining half of the tomato sauce, brown sugar, vinegar, sugar and mustard to a boil. Remove meat loaf from oven. Pour topping mixture over meat loaf and return to oven for an additional 10 minutes.

Devils Tower Lodge
Devils Tower, Wyoming

Seared Day Boat Scallops with Spring Onions, Morelle Mushrooms and English Pea Sauce

Makes 4 servings

12 spring onions, divided
4 T. butter, divided
Salt and pepper to taste
Pinch of sugar
1 1/4 C. fresh peas,
    shelled and blanched
    in salted boiling water

1 C. chicken broth, divided
Fresh Morelle mushrooms,
    cut in half
12 large scallops
1 T. olive oil

To make English Pea Sauce, mince 4 of the spring onions. In a medium saucepan over medium heat, sauté minced spring onions in 2 tablespoons butter, until tender. Add salt, pepper and sugar. Add fresh blanched peas and 3/4 cup chicken broth. Transfer mixture to a blender or food processor and process until smooth. Strain sauce through a fine strainer. In a small sauté pan or skillet, heat mushrooms in 1 tablespoon butter, until tender. Add salt and pepper. Stir in 1/4 cup English Pea Sauce. In a separate sauté pan, heat remaining spring onions in remaining 1 tablespoon butter. Add a pinch of sugar and salt and remaining 1/4 cup chicken broth. In a separate sauté pan, sauté scallops in olive oil and cook until scallops are caramelized on both sides. To serve, ladle remaining hot English Pea sauce into 4 warm bowls. Divide spring onions mixture between the bowls. Place 3 scallops in each bowl. Carefully garnish bowls with mushroom sauce.

The Lodge and Spa at Cordillera
Edwards, Colorado

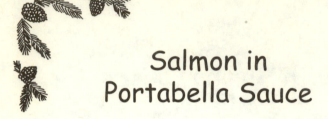

Salmon in Portabella Sauce

2 large (about 10 lbs. each) king salmon filets
2 T. olive oil or butter
2 C. portabella mushrooms

1 C. shallots
2 tsp. tarragon
1 C. white wine
2 C. sour cream

Preheat oven to 375°. In a large oven-safe pan, place salmon filets skin-side down. Bake for 1 hour, until salmon is light orange in color. In a large skillet over low heat, heat olive oil. Add mushrooms, shallots, tarragon and white wine and sauté until cooked throughout. Before serving, add sour cream and stir until heated. Remove salmon from oven and place on serving dish. Pour mushroom mixture over salmon filets. Serve immediately.

Nushagak Salmon Camp Lodge
Anchorage, Alaska

Maple Roasted Salmon with Orange Crème Fraiche on a Bed of Wild Rice

Makes 4 servings

2 C. pure maple syrup
1/2 C. soy sauce
1 T. fresh grated
   gingerroot
4 (8 oz.) salmon filets
1 C. crème fraiche*
1 T. grated orange peel
1 T. Grand Marnier
   liqueur

1 C. wild rice
1 tsp. dried thyme
3 C. water
Pinch of garlic powder
Salt and white pepper
   to taste
Chopped green onions,
   optional

To make marinade, in a 9x13" baking dish, combine maple syrup, soy sauce and grated gingerroot. Place salmon filets in marinade overnight in refrigerator, turning twice. Preheat oven to 350°. To make sauce, combine crème fraiche, orange peel and liqueur. Lightly fold ingredients together and set aside. In an oven-proof dish, combine wild rice, dried thyme, water, garlic powder, salt and white pepper. Bake for 45 minutes, until all liquid has absorbed. Place marinated salmon filets on a lightly greased baking sheet and bake for 12 to 15 minutes. To serve, place 1/4 of the rice mixture on each plate, place salmon over rice and top with a dollop of crème fraiche mixture. If desired, garnish with chopped green onions.

* To make crème fraiche, combine 1/2 cup sour cream and 1/2 cup heavy cream and whip to stiff peaks.

St. Germain Lodge
St. Germain, Wisconsin

Walleye in White Wine

2 C. bread crumbs
1 to 2 T. milk
1 T. finely chopped
    parsley
1 clove garlic, finely
    chopped
1 shallot, finely chopped
1/2 C. plus 3 T. butter,
    softened, divided

Salt and pepper to taste
1 egg yolk
2 small walleye,
    thoroughly cleaned
1 onion, chopped
Dry white wine
1 T. flour

Preheat oven to 350°. In a small bowl, moisten bread crumbs in milk. To make stuffing, in a medium bowl, combine chopped parsley, chopped garlic, chopped shallots and moistened bread crumbs. Mix in 1/2 cup butter, salt, pepper and egg yolk. Stuff walleyes with bread crumb mixture. In a medium saucepan over medium heat, melt 2 tablespoons butter. Sauté chopped onions in butter, until transparent but not browned. Spread cooked onions over the bottom of a greased 9x13" baking dish. Lay stuffed walleyes over onions. Cover with dry white wine. Bake for 30 minutes. Remove pan from oven and pour juices from baking dish into a medium saucepan. Add remaining 1 tablespoon butter and flour to saucepan with juices. Cook over medium heat, until mixture is reduced and thickened. If desired, add a small amount of dry white wine to sauce. Pour sauce over fish in baking dish. Bake for an additional 5 to 10 minutes. Fish is done when it flakes easily with a fork.

Three Seasons Lodge on Otter Tail Lake
Battle Lake, Minnesota

Grilled Flat Iron Steak with Sweet Corn-Shrimp Hash

Makes 4 servings

6 cloves garlic
2 sprigs fresh rosemary
8 sprigs fresh thyme
Zest of 1 lemon
   (about 2 T.)
2 C. plus 2 T. vegetable
   oil, divided
2 lbs. fresh trimmed
   flat iron steak
Salt and pepper
1 small sweet potato,
   peeled and diced

1 small Idaho potato,
   peeled and diced
1 small Poblano pepper, diced
1 small red pepper, diced
1/2 C. chopped scallions
2 ears fresh corn,
   removed from cob
1/2 C. crispy diced bacon
8 large shrimp, sautéed
   and diced
1 C. Zinfandel wine
1 qt. veal stock

In a blender, combine garlic, rosemary, thyme, lemon zest and 2 cups oil. Blend until smooth. Place marinade in a 9x13" baking dish and place steak in marinade. Season with salt and pepper. Marinate in refrigerator for 6 to 12 hours, making sure to fully cover steak. Place marinated steak on a heated grill to cook. Grill to medium rare and set aside. To make Corn-Shrimp Hash, in a large skillet, heat remaining 2 tablespoons oil. Add sweet and Idaho potatoes. Brown potatoes and add diced Poblano peppers, red peppers and scallions. Cook over high heat for 2 to 3 minutes. Fold in corn, diced bacon and diced shrimp. Continue to cook until fully heated. To make sauce, in a stainless steel pan over high heat, reduce wine to 1 tablespoon. Add veal stock and reduce until thickened. Approximately 1 cup should remain. Season with salt and pepper. To serve, place an even amount of Corn-Shrimp Hash on 4 warmed plates. Slice steak into 20 slices. Place 5 slices on each plate. Ladle 4 tablespoons sauce over each serving.

Rough Creek Lodge
Glen Rose, Texas

Northwest Angle
Fried Fish

Walleye filets, or any fish,   2 T. water
   cleaned, cut into pieces   1 C. crushed corn flakes
1 C. flour   1 C. cornmeal
Salt and pepper   1 C. crushed crackers
1 egg, beaten   2 to 4 T. vegetable oil

Cover walleye pieces with flour and sprinkle with salt and pepper. In a small bowl, combine beaten egg and water. In a separate bowl, combine crushed corn flakes, cornmeal and crushed crackers. Place floured walleye pieces in egg mixture, remove and roll in crushed corn flakes mixture. In a large skillet over high heat, heat oil. Place covered walleye pieces in hot oil and fry, being careful not to cook too long, as fish pieces fry very fast. If desired, serve with tartar sauce (page 7).

Variation
To make very crispy fried fish, replace corn flakes, cornmeal and crackers with dry potato buds. Again, be careful not to overcook.

Prothero's Post Resort
Angle Inlet, Minnesota

Breaded Salmon Steaks

4 T. butter, melted
2 tsp. salt
1/2 tsp. paprika

2 C. Italian bread crumbs
3/4 C. dry ranch dressing mix
4 (4" x 4") salmon steaks

In a large bowl or pan, combine melted butter, salt and paprika. In a separate large bowl, combine bread crumbs and ranch dressing mix. Dip salmon steaks in butter mixture and roll in bread crumb mixture. Place salmon steaks on a lightly greased baking sheet and heat under broiler for 5 minutes. Turn salmon steaks and broil for an additional 5 minutes. Serve immediately.

Nushagak Salmon Camp Lodge
Anchorage, Alaska

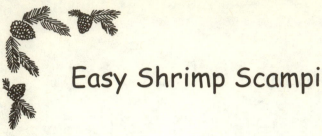

Easy Shrimp Scampi

1/4 C. finely chopped onion	2 lbs. fresh medium shrimp, peeled and deveined
4 cloves garlic, crushed	
4 sprigs fresh parsley, chopped	2 T. lemon juice
3/4 C. butter	Salt and pepper to taste

In a large sauté pan over medium heat, sauté chopped onions, crushed garlic and chopped parsley in butter, until onions are tender. Reduce heat to low and add shrimp. Cook, stirring frequently, for 5 minutes. Remove shrimp with a slotted spoon, place on serving plate and keep warm. Add lemon juice, salt and pepper to ingredients in sauté pan. Let simmer for 2 minutes and pour onion mixture over shrimp on serving plate.

Wikle Lodge
Bryson City, North Carolina

Linguini Nalepa

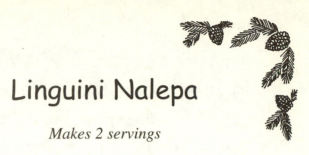

Makes 2 servings

1 clove garlic, crushed	1 carrot, sliced diagonally
1 T. fresh grated gingerroot	1/4 tsp. Szechwan sauce
	1/4 C. white wine
3 T. olive oil	1/2 tsp. soy sauce
1/2 lb. shrimp, peeled and deveined	1/4 tsp. sesame oil
	2 servings cooked linguini
1/4 C. sliced mushrooms	Fresh grated Romano
1/2 C. broccoli florets	cheese, optional

In a medium skillet, sauté crushed garlic and grated gingerroot in olive oil. Add shrimp and sauté just until shrimp turns pink. Remove shrimp and keep warm. Add sliced mushrooms, broccoli and carrots to skillet and cook until tender but crispy. Return shrimp to sauté pan and add Szechwan sauce, white wine, soy sauce and sesame oil. Cook until mixture is heated throughout. Add cooked linguini to pan and toss all together. If desired, sprinkle fresh grated Romano cheese over linguini.

Buffalo Run Lodge
Arbovale, West Virginia

Millbrook Farm Venison North Country Stew and Sautéed Ruby Swiss Chard on Parsnip Puree

North Country Stew

6 T. vegetable oil, divided
2 large onions, thinly
   sliced
1/2 lb. shitake
   mushrooms, stemmed
   and quartered
1/2 C. flour

Salt and pepper to taste
1 lb. Millbrook Farm
   venison leg meat, cleaned
   and diced
2 C. red wine
2 qts. veal stock

In a Dutch oven over medium heat, heat 3 tablespoons oil. Add onions after 30 seconds and sauté until light golden brown. Add mushrooms and sauté until light brown, about 2 to 3 minutes, stirring constantly. Remove onions and mushrooms from Dutch oven. Add remaining 3 tablespoon oil and heat for 30 seconds. In a small bowl, combine flour, salt and pepper. Dust diced venison with seasoned flour and shake off excess. Brown venison on all sides in Dutch oven, stirring occasionally. Add onions and mushrooms and deglaze with red wine. Reduce red wine by half and add veal stock just to cover. Season with salt and pepper. Place in a 275° oven for 4 to 5 hours. Check tenderness of meat after 4 hours. Meat is finished when tender and not chewy.

Parsnip Puree

1 lb. parsnips, peeled
1 qt. whole milk

Salt and pepper

Roughly chop parsnips, including cores, to a uniform size. In a medium saucepan over medium heat, place chopped

(continued on next page)

78

parsnips. Cover with whole milk and a pinch of salt. Bring mixture to a simmer, heating until parsnips are tender. Strain parsnips, reserving milk. In a blender, place parsnips and add 1/3 of the reserved milk. Puree until smooth. Puree should be the consistency of mashed potatoes. If puree is too thick, add more milk. Season with salt and pepper.

Seared Loin of Millbrook Farm Venison

6 (4 oz.) venison loins, cleaned

Salt and pepper
2 T. vegetable oil

Preheat oven to 400°. Season each side of venison with salt and pepper. Heat an oven-safe sauté pan over medium heat for 1 minute. Add oil to hot pan. Brown venison evenly on all sides. Place sauté pan with venison in oven for about 8 minutes. Remove from oven and place cooked venison loins on a warm plate. Let rest for 3 minutes before cutting each portion into 3 slices.

Sautéed Ruby Swiss Chard

2 T. vegetable oil
2 bunches Ruby Swiss chard, washed, dried and stemmed

1 T. chopped garlic
2 T. white wine
Salt and pepper

In a large sauté pan over high heat, heat oil. When oil is hot, add Ruby Swiss chard and chopped garlic, stirring constantly. After 30 seconds, add white wine to deglaze pan. Season with salt and pepper.

To serve
Spoon a generous amount of hot Parsnip Puree into the center of each serving plate. With the back of a spoon, form a well in the center of puree. Spoon hot North Country Stew in the well of parsnip puree. Place enough Sautéed Ruby Swiss Chard to cover stew. Place 3 slices Millbrook Farm Venison Loin neatly on top of Ruby Swiss Chard on each plate. Drizzle with remaining stew.

Lake Placid Lodge
Lake Placid, New York

Red Pepper Pasta Primavera

Makes 6 servings

1/2 T. dried basil
1/2 T. dried parsley
   flakes
1 medium to large red
   pepper, chopped
1/2 C. mayonnaise
2 T. grated Parmesan
   cheese
1 T. lemon juice
1/2 tsp. salt
1/8 tsp. Tabasco sauce
1/8 tsp. pepper
8 C. water

2 T. olive oil
16 oz. fettuccine or
   linguine pasta
2 large carrots, cut into
   long thin strips
1 medium onion, cut
   into wedges
1 medium zucchini, cut
   into long thin strips
10 oz. cooked chicken
   or turkey breast,
   cut into strips

In a blender or food processor, combine basil, parsley flakes, chopped red peppers, mayonnaise, grated Parmesan cheese, lemon juice, salt, Tabasco sauce and pepper. Puree until smooth and set aside. In a large pot, combine water and olive oil and bring to a boil. Cook pasta for 6 minutes. Add carrots and onions and boil for an additional 2 minutes. Add zucchini and boil for 2 more minutes, until pasta is done, but not mushy. Drain pasta and vegetables and return to pot. Add blended mixture, cooked chicken or turkey strips and toss until evenly incorporated. Cook over very low heat until heated throughout, tossing occasionally. Serve immediately.

Rocky Mountain Lodge & Cabins
Cascade, Colorado

Wild Rice Soup

1/2 C. wild rice
3 1/4 C. water, divided
1/2 tsp. salt
1 medium onion,
   chopped

2 T. margarine
2 cans cream of potato
   soup
1 qt. milk
1 lb. Velveeta cheese, cubed

In a medium saucepan over medium heat, cook wild rice in 1 1/4 cups water. Add salt and bring to a boil. Let simmer for 40 to 50 minutes. Drain and rinse. In a separate saucepan over low heat, sauté chopped onions in margarine until tender. Add remaining 2 cups water, cream of potato soup and milk. Increase heat to medium, stirring occasionally. When mixture is hot, add cubed Velveeta cheese. When cheese has melted, stir in cooked wild rice. Serve warm.

Cedar Rapids Lodge
Tenstrike, Minnesota

Simply Chic
Seafood Bisque

1/2 lb. white fish
1/2 C. chicken or
   vegetable broth
1/4 lb. fresh shrimp,
   peeled, deveined,
   cooked and chilled
1/4 lb. fresh or imitation
   crabmeat

4 C. low-salt tomato soup
1 1/2 T. curry
2 C. evaporated milk
   or 1 1/2 C. sour cream
3 T. fresh lemon juice
1 tsp. nutmeg
Lemon slices and dried
   parsley flakes, optional

In a large skillet over medium heat, lightly sauté white fish in chicken or vegetable broth. In a large bowl, combine sautéed white fish, cooked shrimp, crabmeat, tomato soup, curry, evaporated milk, lemon juice and nutmeg. Place mixture in a large non-aluminum soup pot over medium heat. Heat until soup is slightly steaming, being careful not to boil. Can be served either hot or chilled. If desired, garnish with lemon slices and a pinch of dried parsley flakes.

Pond Mountain Lodge
Eureka Springs, Arkansas

Venison Chili

1 lb. cubed venison
1 pkg. chili seasoning,
    divided
1 (32) oz. bottle spicy
    hot V8 juice
1 (8 oz.) can diced
    tomatoes with green
    chilies
1 (8 oz.) can pork n' beans
    in juice

1 (8 oz.) can chili beans
    in juice
1 clove garlic, minced
1 small onion, diced,
    divided
8 oz. shredded Colby
    Jack cheese
1 green pepper, diced
1 red pepper, diced

In a large saucepan over medium heat, brown venison and drain off fat. Stir in half of the chili seasoning. Mix well and place in a large crock pot. Add V8 juice, diced tomatoes with green chilies, pork n' beans in juice, chili beans in juice and minced garlic. Add 1/3 of the diced onions and remaining half of the chili seasoning. Mix well and turn crock pot on high. After 40 minutes, mix again and reduce crock pot to low. Cook for 2 to 4 hours. Place desired amount of remaining diced onions, shredded Colby Jack cheese, diced green peppers and diced red peppers into individual serving bowls. Ladle chili over ingredients in bowls.

Three Seasons Lodge on Otter Tail Lake
Battle Lake, Minnesota

Rueben Soup

Makes 6 servings

1/2 C. chopped onions	3/4 C. sauerkraut,
1/2 C. sliced celery	rinsed and drained
2 T. butter or margarine	2 C. half n' half
1 C. chicken broth	2 C. chopped corned beef
1 C. beef broth	1 C. shredded Swiss cheese
1/2 tsp. baking soda	Salt and pepper
2 T. cornstarch	Rye croutons, optional
2 T. cold water	

In a large saucepan over medium heat, sauté onions and celery in butter until tender. Add chicken broth, beef broth and baking soda. In a small bowl, combine cornstarch and cold water. Add cornstarch mixture to onions mixture and bring to a boil. Boil for 2 minutes, stirring occasionally. Reduce heat and add drained sauerkraut, half n' half and chopped corned beef. Let mixture simmer, stirring occasionally, for 15 minutes. Add shredded Swiss cheese, heating until cheese is melted. Add salt and pepper to taste. If desired, garnish with rye croutons.

Boyd Lodge
Crosslake, Minnesota

Broccoli Cheese Soup

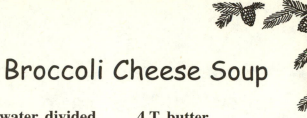

6 1/2 C. water, divided
1 box frozen chopped
   broccoli, thawed
1 onion, chopped
1 small box Velveeta
   cheese, cubed

4 T. butter
1 C. milk
1 C. half n' half
1/2 C. flour

In a large soup pot, bring 6 cups water to a boil. Add chopped broccoli and chopped onions and cook for 10 minutes. Stir in cubed Velveeta cheese and butter. Add milk and half n' half and mix until cheese is melted. In a small bowl, combine flour and remaining 1/2 cup water, mixing until smooth. Stir flour mixture into soup.

Wikle Lodge
Bryson City, North Carolina

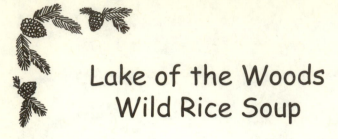

Lake of the Woods
Wild Rice Soup

3/4 C. wild rice
1/4 C. chopped onion
3/4 C. chopped celery
1/2 C. sliced carrots
2 T. oil or bacon
   drippings
2 strips crispy fried
   bacon, crumbled
1 can chicken broth
1 can cream of
   mushroom soup
1 soup can 2% milk

2 C. water
1 (4 oz.) can mushrooms
   in juice
1/2 to 3/4 tsp. seasoning salt
1/2 C. Velveeta Light cheese
2 medium potatoes, cubed
Pepper to taste
1/4 tsp. garlic powder
1/2 tsp. dried thyme
1/4 tsp. Mrs. Dash
   original blend

Thoroughly rinse wild rice under cool water. Fill a large pot with water and boil rice for 30 minutes. Drain rice and set aside. In a medium skillet over medium heat, sauté onions, celery and carrots in oil. In a large soup pot, place cooked and drained wild rice, sautéed onions, celery and carrots, crumbled bacon, chicken broth, cream of mushroom soup, milk, water, mushrooms in juice, seasoning salt, Velveeta cheese, cubed potatoes, pepper, garlic powder, dried thyme and Mrs. Dash original blend. Lightly stir ingredients until combined. Simmer over low heat for 30 minutes.

Prothero's Post Resort
Angle Inlet, Minnesota

Grandma Mindala's Chicken Noodle Soup

5 to 6 lbs. whole
   chicken breasts or
   wings
4 to 5 chicken bouillon
   cubes
1 small can tomatoes,
   drained, divided
3 large onions, chopped

4 large carrots, chopped
4 stalks celery, sliced
4 to 5 tsp. fresh chopped
   parsley
1 bunch celery tops, chopped
Salt and pepper to taste
2 tsp. minced garlic
Noodles, cooked

In a large pot, boil chicken breasts or wings in enough water to cover chicken. Add chicken bouillon cubes and half of the drained tomatoes. Cook chicken until very tender, remove from water and drain. Let chicken cool and remove skin and bones. Add chopped onions, chopped carrots, sliced celery, chopped parsley, chopped celery tops and remaining half can of tomatoes to pot. Cook vegetables in chicken broth over medium heat. Add cleaned chicken, salt, pepper and minced garlic. Prepare desired amount of noodles by cooking in a separate pan of boiling water. Ladle soup into bowl and add cooked noodles just before serving.

Note
Light-colored chicken will make better soup, as will fresh chicken, instead of chicken that has been previously frozen.

Johnson's Allagash Lodge
Mapleton, Maine

Judy's Cuban Black Bean Chili

2 lbs. ground beef
1 onion, diced
1 green pepper, diced
3 cloves garlic, crushed
3 carrots, finely grated
4 cans black beans,
   drained
1 (28 to 32 oz.) can
   crushed tomatoes
2 (40 oz.) cans peeled
   and diced tomatoes

Juice of 3 limes
Dash of Tabasco sauce
   or Louisiana Hot Sauce
1 T. cumin
1 T. garlic powder
1/2 to 1 C. beer, any kind
Sour cream, lime slices
   and fresh mint leaves,
   optional

In a large pot, sauté ground beef until fully browned and drain off fat. Add diced onions, diced peppers and sauté until lightly browned. Add crushed garlic and grated carrots. Sauté for an additional 5 to 8 minutes, until well blended. Add drained black beans, crushed tomatoes, diced tomatoes, lime juice, Tabasco sauce, cumin and garlic powder. Let mixture simmer for about 35 minutes. Mix in beer until chili reaches desired thickness. If desired, serve chili with a dollop of sour cream, slice of lime and fresh mint leaves.

Variation
Can replace cans of black beans with 1 pound dry black beans cooked in chicken broth.

Pond Mountain Lodge
Eureka Springs, Arkansas

Desserts

Tira-Moose-Su

6 eggs
1 T. vanilla
1 1/4 C. sugar, divided
16 oz. mascarpone cheese
6 egg whites

1/2 C. Kahlua liqueur
1/2 C. espresso
Soft lady fingers
Cocoa powder

In a double boiler, whisk together eggs, vanilla and 1 cup sugar. Whisk continuously until water just starts to boil, being careful not to cook the eggs. Immediately pour into a mixing bowl. Beat at medium high speed until cool and fluffy. Gradually add cheese. Beat at low speed, being careful not to overmix, as cheese will separate. Set aside. In a separate bowl, beat egg whites and remaining 1/4 cup sugar to a medium peak. Fold egg white mixture into cheese mixture to form custard. In a small bowl, combine Kahlua and espresso. In individual sorbet cups, a large round glass bowl or a 9x13" baking dish, layer lady fingers along the bottom. Brush Kahlua mixture generously over lady fingers and dust with cocoa powder. Add enough custard just to cover lady fingers. Repeat with another layer of lady fingers, Kahlua mixture, cocoa powder and custard. Sprinkle more cocoa powder generously over top layer of custard. Refrigerate at least 2 to 3 hours. Carefully dip a moose cookie cutter, or any other shape, into the custard. The cookie cutter should leave an impression in the mousse. Can be prepared 2 days prior to serving.

Note
The US FDA does not recommend eating raw eggs.

Moose Meadow Lodge
Waterbury, Vermont

Caramel Rhubarb
Bread Pudding

4 eggs, beaten
2 1/2 C. milk
1 tsp. vanilla
1/2 C. brown sugar

3 C. cubed day old bread
Cinnamon
2 C. diced rhubarb

Grease a 9x9" pan and set aside. In a large bowl, combine beaten eggs, milk, vanilla and brown sugar. Spread bread cubes over bottom of prepared pan. Pour egg and brown sugar mixture over bread cubes. Sprinkle generously with cinnamon. Spread diced rhubarb over cinnamon in pan. Refrigerate overnight. Preheat oven to 350°. Bake for 45 minutes, until center of pudding is set.

Topping

2 T. butter
2 T. instant vanilla
   pudding mix

2 T. brown sugar
Milk

In a medium saucepan over medium heat, melt butter. Stir in vanilla pudding mix and brown sugar. Pour in enough milk to thin out the mixture. Pour topping over hot bread pudding.

Variation
May substitute diced apples for the rhubarb.

Evergreen Lodge
Boulder Junction, Wisconsin

Maple Crème Brulee

Makes 4 servings

2 C. heavy whipping
  cream
1/2 vanilla bean, split
  lengthwise

5 egg yolks
1/8 C. plus 2 T. maple
  syrup
Sugar for topping

Preheat oven to 325°. In a heavy saucepan over medium heat, heat heavy cream. Scrape seeds from vanilla bean half and add to cream, along with vanilla pod. Bring cream just to a boil and remove from heat. In a medium bowl, combine egg yolks and maple syrup, whisking until smooth and slightly foamy. Gradually add hot cream to egg mixture, whisking constantly. Once all cream has been added, strain mixture through a fine sieve and set aside. Place four 6-ounce custard dishes in a large roasting pan. Ladle cream mixture into custard dishes. Add enough warm water to roasting pan to reach less than halfway up the sides of the custard dishes. Place roaster pan in oven for 40 minutes. Check if custard is firm by gently shaking the roasting pan. The custard should be movable, but not too loose. Remove custard dishes from water and cool to room temperature. Chill in refrigerator for a few hours. Before serving, sprinkle tops of custard with sugar. Melt and brown the sugar either by placing custard cups under a broiler or by using a propane kitchen torch. Serve immediately.

Snowbird Mountain Lodge
Robbinsville, North Carolina

Pear Frittata

2 pears, firm and ripe
2 T. butter or margarine
6 large eggs
1/3 C. milk
1/4 C. flour
1 T. sugar

1 tsp. vanilla
1/4 tsp. salt
1/4 C. cream cheese,
   whipped, divided
1 to 2 T. brown sugar

Preheat oven to 425°. Peel and cut pears into 1/2" pieces. In a 9" or 10" non-stick pan, melt butter over medium heat. Add pears to pan, heating until pears are lightly browned. In a medium bowl, combine eggs, milk, flour, sugar, vanilla and salt. Pour mixture over pears. Bake for 8 to 12 minutes. Remove from oven and place some of the pear mixture on each plate. Spoon some of the whipped cream cheese over each serving. Sprinkle with brown sugar.

Devils Tower Lodge
Devils Tower, Wyoming

Apple Crisp

Apples, peeled, cored and sliced	1/2 C. butter, softened
	3/4 C. flour
2 tsp. cinnamon	1 C. brown sugar

Preheat oven to 350°. Grease a microwave-safe 8x8" pan. Cut enough apples to fill the pan with a heaping amount. Microwave apples for 5 minutes and drain excess juice. Stir in cinnamon. In a medium bowl, use a pastry cutter to combine butter, flour and brown sugar. Sprinkle mixture over apples in pan. Bake for 30 minutes, until apples are tender. Can be served warm or cold.

Lazy Cloud Lodge
Fontana, Wisconsin

Blueberry Crisp with Walnut Streusel Topping

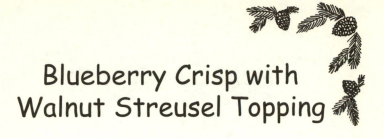

Makes 6 to 8 servings

1 1/2 C. flour	1 C. chopped walnuts
1 1/4 C. sugar, divided	8 C. fresh blueberries
2 1/2 tsp. cinnamon, divided	2 T. lemon juice
10 T. butter or margarine, cut into pieces	1 1/2 T. cornstarch

In a large bowl, whisk together flour, 1/2 cup sugar and 1 teaspoon cinnamon. Add pieces of butter and mix with fingers or a spoon. Press mixture together until moist clumps form. Mix in chopped walnuts. Cover and chill in refrigerator. Preheat oven to 375°. In a greased 9x13" baking dish, place blueberries. Add remaining 3/4 cup sugar, lemon juice, cornstarch and remaining 1 1/2 teaspoons cinnamon to baking dish. Gently toss all together and spread evenly over bottom of dish. Sprinkle flour and walnuts mixture over ingredients in baking dish. Bake about 50 minutes, until topping is browned and blueberry filling is bubbling.

Prothero's Post Resort
Angle Inlet, Minnesota

Delicious Scones

2 C. flour

1/2 C. sugar

1/2 tsp. salt

1/2 tsp. baking soda

1/2 C. shortening

1 egg

1 C. sour cream

Fruits or jam, optional

Preheat oven to 400°. In a large bowl, combine flour, sugar, salt, baking soda and shortening. Mix with a fork until small clumps appear. Add egg and sour cream and knead until well mixed. Flatten dough. If desired, layer currants, raisins, apple slices sprinkled with cinnamon and sugar, or jam over the dough. Fold dough in half to enclose fruits or jam. Cut dough into wedges and place on a greased baking sheet. Bake for 15 minutes.

Point Au Roche Lodge
Plattsburgh, New York

Turtle Cookies

1/2 C. butter, melted
2/3 C. sugar
6 T. cocoa powder
1/2 tsp. vanilla

1/2 tsp. salt, optional
1 C. plus 1 T. flour
2 eggs, beaten
Powdered sugar

Preheat and lightly grease a waffle iron to medium heat. In a medium bowl, combine melted butter, sugar, cocoa powder, vanilla, salt, flour and beaten eggs. Mix until well blended. Drop 1 teaspoon dough every 2" on hot waffle iron. Close waffle iron and bake for 45 seconds to 1 minute. Remove cookies and sprinkle with powdered sugar.

Pike Point Resort & Lodge
Tenstrike, Minnesota

97

Shannon's Snickerdoodles

1/2 C. butter, softened
1 1/2 C. plus 5 T. sugar,
   divided
1 1/2 tsp. vanilla
2 eggs

1/4 C. milk
3 1/2 C. flour
1 tsp. baking soda
1/2 C. finely chopped walnuts
2 T. cinnamon

Line a baking sheet with parchment paper and set aside. In a large bowl, combine butter and 1 1/2 cups sugar. Add vanilla, eggs and milk and mix well. In a separate bowl, combine flour and baking soda. Pour butter and sugar mixture over dry ingredients and mix until well combined. Blend in finely chopped walnuts. Form dough into a log shape and cover with plastic wrap. Chill in refrigerator for 20 to 25 minutes. Preheat oven to 375°. In a separate bowl, combine remaining 5 tablespoons sugar and cinnamon. Remove dough from refrigerator and roll into 1" balls. Roll balls in cinnamon and sugar mixture and place on prepared baking sheet. Flatten each cookie with the back of a fork. Bake for 10 to 12 minutes, until lightly browned.

Minnewaska Lodge
Gardiner, New York

Sour Cream
Rhubarb Bars

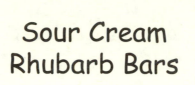

1 1/2 C. quick oats
1 C. brown sugar
1 C. margarine, softened
1 3/4 C. flour
1 tsp. baking soda

4 egg yolks
2 T. cornstarch
1 1/2 C. sugar
2 C. sour cream
2 C. chopped rhubarb

Preheat oven to 350°. In a large bowl, combine oats, brown sugar, margarine, flour and baking soda. Press half of the mixture into the bottom of a greased 9x13" baking dish. Bake for 10 to 15 minutes. To make filling, in a large saucepan, combine egg yolks, cornstarch, sugar, sour cream and chopped rhubarb. Heat mixture over low heat until thickened. Pour mixture over hot crust in pan. Sprinkle remaining half of the crust mixture over filling. Bake for an additional 20 minutes. Let cool before cutting into bars.

Boyd Lodge
Crosslake, Minnesota

Special K Bars

1/2 C. sugar	3/4 C. peanut butter
1/2 C. light corn syrup	1 (6 oz.) pkg. chocolate chips
3 C. Special K cereal	1 (6 oz.) pkg. butterscotch
1 tsp. vanilla	chips

In a large saucepan over medium heat, bring sugar and corn syrup to a boil. Add cereal, vanilla and peanut butter and mix until evenly blended. Pour mixture into a lightly greased 9x13" baking dish. In a medium microwave-safe bowl, combine chocolate chips and butterscotch chips. Microwave for 30 second periods, until chips are melted. Mix well and spread evenly over ingredients in pan. Chill in refrigerator. Cut into squares before serving.

Cedar Rapids Lodge
Tenstrike, Minnesota

Peanut Butter Swirl Brownies

1 tsp. vegetable oil
1 1/2 C. butter, melted
3 1/2 C. sugar, divided
1 T. plus 1 tsp. vanilla,
    divided
8 eggs, divided
1 1/2 C. flour
1 C. cocoa powder
3/4 tsp. baking powder

3/4 tsp. salt
1 C. chopped walnuts,
    optional
1 C. chocolate chips
12 oz. cream cheese,
    softened
1 C. peanut butter
4 T. milk

Preheat oven to 350°. Line a glass 9x13" baking dish with aluminum foil. Drizzle vegetable oil over foil and spread evenly. In a large bowl, combine melted butter, 3 cups sugar and 1 tablespoon vanilla. Add 6 eggs, one at a time, beating well after each addition. In a separate bowl, combine flour, cocoa powder, baking powder and salt. Pour butter and sugar mixture over dry ingredients and mix well. Add chopped walnuts and chocolate chips. Reserve 1 1/2 cups batter and set aside. Pour remaining batter into prepared pan. In a separate bowl, beat cream cheese, peanut butter, milk, remaining 2 eggs, remaining 1/2 cup sugar and remaining 1 teaspoon vanilla at medium speed, until creamy. Pour peanut butter batter over chocolate batter in pan. Pour reserved 1 1/2 cups chocolate batter over top. Use a knife to swirl the two batters together. Bake for 35 to 40 minutes or until a toothpick inserted in center comes out clean.

Minnewaska Lodge
Gardiner, New York

101

Chocolate Mint Brownies

3/4 C. butter or
margarine, softened
1 1/3 C. sugar
1 1/2 tsp. vanilla
1/2 tsp. peppermint
extract

3 eggs
3/4 C. flour
1/2 C. cocoa powder
1/2 tsp. baking powder
1/2 tsp. salt
3/4 C. chocolate chips

Preheat oven to 350°. In a large bowl, combine butter, sugar, vanilla and peppermint extract. Add eggs and beat well. In a separate bowl, combine flour, cocoa powder, baking powder and salt. Add flour mixture to eggs mixture and mix until well blended. Stir in chocolate chips. Pour batter into a greased 9x13" baking dish. Bake for 25 minutes, until brownies pull away from sides of pan with a knife. Let cool before cutting into squares.

Buffalo Run Lodge
Arbovale, West Virginia

Texas Delight

1/2 C. butter, softened
1 C. flour
1 C. chopped walnuts
1 (8 oz.) pkg. cream
   cheese, softened
1 1/2 C. powdered sugar
1/2 tsp. vanilla
1 (16 oz.) container frozen
   whipped topping,
   thawed, divided

1 small pkg. instant
   vanilla pudding mix
1 small pkg. instant
   chocolate pudding mix
3 C. milk
1 Hershey's chocolate bar

Preheat oven to 350°. In a medium bowl, combine butter, flour and chopped walnuts. Mix well and pat mixture into the bottom of a lightly greased 9x13" baking dish. Bake for 15 minutes, remove from oven and let cool. In a separate bowl, combine cream cheese, powdered sugar, vanilla and half of the whipped topping. Mix well and spread over cooled crust in pan. Chill in refrigerator. In a separate bowl, combine vanilla pudding mix, chocolate pudding mix and milk. Spread over cream cheese layer. Spread remaining half of the whipped topping over pudding layer. Grate chocolate bar over whipped topping. Refrigerate, uncovered, until ready to serve.

Balsam Beach Resort & RV Park
Bemidji, Minnesota

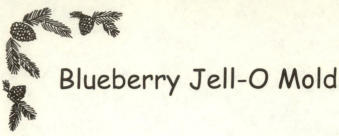

Blueberry Jell-O Mold

1 (6 oz.) pkg. raspberry
  Jell-O mix
2 C. hot water
1 can blueberry pie
  filling
1 (16 oz.) can crushed
  pineapple in syrup

8 oz. frozen whipped
  topping, thawed
1 C. sour cream
1/4 C. sugar
Chopped nuts, optional

In a medium bowl, combine raspberry Jell-O mix and hot water. Mix well and add blueberry pie filling and crushed pineapple in syrup. Blend well and pour into a glass 9x13" baking dish. Chill in refrigerator. In a separate bowl, combine whipped topping, sour cream and sugar. If desired, stir in chopped nuts. When Jell-O has set, spread whipped topping mixture evenly over Jell-O.

Pike Point Resort & Lodge
Tenstrike, Minnesota

Orchard Pear Tart

Makes 8 to 10 servings

1 (10") sweet tart pastry
6 T. butter
1 1/2 eggs (beat 2nd egg
 and use only half)
1/2 C. plus 1 T. sugar
3 T. flour, sifted
4 ripe pears, peeled and
 cut in half lengthwise

5 C. cold water
2 T. lemon juice
1/2 C. apricot preserves
1 T. pear liqueur
1/4 C. powdered sugar

Line a 10" round pan with sweet tart pastry. Cover with plastic wrap and refrigerate for 1 hour. To make custard filling, in a medium saucepan over medium heat, melt butter until light brown. Remove from heat and let cool 5 minutes. In a medium bowl, whisk eggs with sugar. Whisk in flour and melted butter and set aside. Preheat oven to 375°. Remove cores and seeds from pear halves. In a large bowl, combine cold water and lemon juice. Place pear halves in water mixture. Remove from water and place on paper towels to dry. Using a sharp knife, beginning at the narrow end of the pear with the knife at a 45° angle, cut each pear crosswise into 1/8" slices. Carefully slide a thin spatula under each cut pear and transfer to pastry lined tart pan, pointing narrow end of each pear toward center. Slightly fan the pear slices. Pour prepared custard filling in the empty spaces around the pears, but not over pears. Custard should only fill halfway up side of tart. Bake for 20 minutes. Reduce heat to 350° and bake an additional 40 to 50 minutes, until custard is fully cooked. Remove from oven and let cool. To make glaze, in a separate saucepan over low heat, heat apricot preserves until melted. Strain to remove pieces of fruit. Stir in pear liqueur. Brush a thin coating of glaze over pears in cooled tart. Lightly sift powdered sugar over tart.

Mountain Home Lodge
Leavenworth, Washington

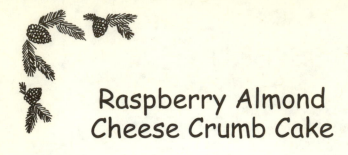

Raspberry Almond Cheese Crumb Cake

1 1/2 C. flour
1 C. old fashioned oats
1 C. sugar, divided
3/4 C. butter, softened
1/2 C. sour cream
2 eggs, divided

1/2 tsp. baking soda
8 oz. cream cheese, softened
1 tsp. almond extract
3/4 C. raspberry preserves
1/3 C. slivered almonds

Preheat oven to 350°. In a large bowl, combine flour, oats, 3/4 cup sugar and butter with a pastry blender, until mixture is crumbly. Reserve 1 cup of crumb mixture and set aside. Add sour cream, 1 egg and baking soda to remaining crumb mixture. Blend well and spread mixture evenly over the bottom of a greased 9x9" pan. In a separate bowl, combine cream cheese, remaining 1/4 cup sugar, almond extract and remaining egg until smooth. Pour cream cheese mixture over batter in pan. Top with an even layer of raspberry preserves. Mix reserved crumb mixture with slivered almonds and sprinkle generously over raspberry preserves. Bake for 45 to 50 minutes or until a toothpick inserted in center comes out clean. Let cool completely before serving.

Minnewaska Lodge
Gardiner, New York

Alamoosook Crumb Apple Pie

3 to 4 apples, peeled,
   cored and diced
1/2 tsp. salt
1 1/4 C. sugar, divided

1 tsp. cinnamon
1 (9") unbaked pie crust
3/4 C. flour
1/3 C. butter, softened

Preheat oven to 375°. In a medium bowl, combine diced apples, salt, 3/4 cup sugar and cinnamon. Mix until evenly blended and pour into pie crust. In a separate bowl, combine remaining 1/2 cup sugar, flour and butter with a pastry blender. Sprinkle flour mixture over apples in pie crust. Bake for 15 minutes. Reduce heat to 350° and bake an additional 45 minutes.

Alamoosook Lodge
Orland, Maine

Chocolate Sundae Pudding Cake

Makes 4 to 6 servings

1 C. flour
2/3 C. plus 1/4 C.
   sugar, divided
5 T. cocoa powder,
   divided
2 tsp. baking powder
3/8 tsp. salt, divided
1/2 C. milk

1/2 C. chopped nuts
2 T. butter or
   margarine, melted
2 tsp. vanilla, divided
1/2 C. brown sugar
1 C. boiling water
French vanilla ice cream,
   optional

Preheat oven to 350°. Grease four to six 2-cup ramekins and set aside. In a large mixing bowl, combine flour, 2/3 cup sugar, 2 tablespoons cocoa powder, baking powder and 1/4 teaspoon salt and set aside. In a small mixing bowl, combine milk, chopped nuts, melted butter and 1 teaspoon vanilla. Add to dry ingredients and mix until well blended. Pour mixture into prepared ramekins. In a separate bowl, combine brown sugar, remaining 1/4 cup sugar, remaining 3 tablespoons cocoa powder, remaining 1 teaspoon vanilla and remaining 1/8 teaspoon salt. Sprinkle mixture evenly over batter. Pour boiling water evenly over each ramekin. Bake for 30 minutes. If desired, serve with French vanilla ice cream.

Rocky Mountain Lodge & Cabins
Cascade, Colorado

Peach Cake

6 C. water
5 to 6 fresh peaches
3/4 C. butter, softened
1 C. plus 2 tsp. sugar,
    divided
3 eggs

2 tsp. vanilla
1 1/2 C. flour
1 1/2 tsp. baking powder
1/4 tsp. salt
2 T. lemon juice

Preheat oven to 350°. Thoroughly grease a 9x9" pan and set aside. In a large saucepan over medium heat, bring water to a rolling boil. Add peaches to boiling water for about 30 seconds. Using a slotted spoon, remove peaches from water and carefully skin peaches with a knife. Cut peaches into slices and set aside. In a large bowl, cream together butter and 1 cup sugar. Add eggs and vanilla and mix well. In a separate bowl, combine flour, baking powder and salt. Pour butter and sugar mixture into dry ingredients and mix well. Pour batter into prepared pan and top with sliced peaches, arranged in a spiral. Lightly sprinkle tops of peaches with lemon juice and remaining 2 teaspoons sugar. Bake for 50 to 60 minutes, until golden brown.

Minnewaska Lodge
Gardiner, New York

Coffee Cake
with Blueberries

4 C. flour
1 C. sugar
2 T. baking powder
1/2 tsp. salt
2 eggs

1 1/2 C. milk
2/3 C. vegetable oil
1 1/2 C. fresh or frozen
   blueberries

Preheat oven to 350°. In a large bowl, combine flour, sugar, baking powder and salt. In a separate bowl, beat eggs, milk and vegetable oil until smooth. Stir egg mixture into flour mixture, blending just until moistened. Fold in blueberries. Transfer mixture to a greased 9x13" baking dish. Bake for 24 minutes.

Variation
For a crumbly topping, combine 1 cup brown sugar, 1/4 cup flour, 1 tablespoon cinnamon and enough butter to make topping moist and crumbly. Place topping on coffee cake before baking. Or, combine 1 cup powdered sugar and enough milk to make a thin frosting. Spread over cake after baking.

Duck Inn
Whitefish, Montana

Bumbleberry Cheesecake

3/4 lb. butter, melted
2 C. graham cracker
   crumbs
3 C. sugar, divided
1 1/2 lbs. cream cheese,
   softened

1 tsp. vanilla
3 eggs
1 egg yolk
5 oz. bumbleberry spread

Preheat oven to 300°. In a large bowl, combine melted butter, graham cracker crumbs and 1 cup sugar. Press mixture into the bottom and up sides of a greased 10" springform pan. Bake for 20 minutes, remove from oven and let cool. To make filling, in a blender or food processor, combine cream cheese, remaining 2 cups sugar and vanilla. Add eggs and egg yolk, one at a time, beating well after each addition. Mix well and transfer to a large bowl. Fold in bumbleberry spread and pour mixture into cooled graham cracker crust. To bake cheesecake, place springform pan in a large pan of hot water for 1 1/2 hours. Remove from water and chill overnight in refrigerator.

Variation
To make a Peanut Butter Cheesecake, replace bumbleberry spread with 10 ounces crunchy peanut butter and blend in food processor with filling ingredients before adding eggs.

St. Germain Lodge
St. Germain, Wisconsin

111

Hot Milk Cake

4 eggs
2 C. sugar
2 C. flour
2 tsp. baking powder
1 C. butter or margarine

1 C. milk
2 tsp. vanilla (or 1 tsp. vanilla and 1 tsp. lemon or almond extract)

Preheat oven to 350°. In a large bowl, beat eggs and sugar until creamy. Add flour and baking powder and mix well. In a small saucepan over medium heat, bring butter and milk to a boil. Add hot milk mixture to flour mixture and stir until well combined. Blend in vanilla. Pour batter into a greased and floured tube pan. Bake for 45 minutes.

Wikle Lodge
Bryson City, North Carolina

Baked Apple Crumb Cake

3/4 C. butter, softened, divided
1 C. sugar
2 eggs
4 tsp. vanilla, divided
6 T. low-fat plain yogurt
2 1/2 C. flour, divided

1/2 tsp. baking soda
2 tsp. baking powder
3 tsp. cinnamon, divided
1/4 tsp. salt
4 C. sliced apples
4 T. brown sugar

Preheat oven to 350°. Thoroughly grease a 9x9" pan and set aside. In a large bowl, combine 1/2 cup butter and sugar. Add eggs, 3 teaspoons vanilla and plain yogurt and mix well. In a separate bowl, combine 2 cups flour, baking soda, baking powder, 1 teaspoon cinnamon and salt. Pour butter and sugar mixture over dry ingredients and mix well. Spread mixture evenly into prepared pan. In a separate bowl, combine sliced apples, 1 teaspoon cinnamon and remaining 1 teaspoon vanilla, until apples are evenly coated. Arrange apples over batter in pan. In a separate bowl, using a pastry blender, cut remaining 1/4 cup butter into remaining 1/2 cup flour, brown sugar and remaining 1 teaspoon cinnamon. Sprinkle crumb mixture over apples in pan. Bake for 30 to 35 minutes or until a toothpick inserted in center comes out clean.

Minnewaska Lodge
Gardiner, New York

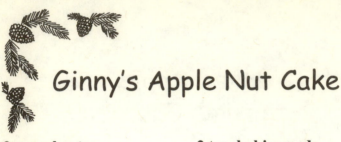

Ginny's Apple Nut Cake

2 eggs, beaten
2 C. sugar
1 tsp. vanilla
1/2 C. oil
2 C. flour

2 tsp. baking soda
2 tsp. cinnamon
3/4 tsp. salt
1 C. chopped walnuts
4 C. finely diced apples

Preheat oven to 325°. In a large bowl, combine eggs, sugar and vanilla. Add oil and beat until smooth. Sift in flour, baking soda, cinnamon and salt. Add chopped walnuts and diced apples and mix well. Place mixture in a greased and floured 9x13" baking dish. Bake for 1 hour. Remove from oven and let cool. If desired, cover cake with Lemon Cream Cheese Icing. Store cake in refrigerator.

Lemon Cream Cheese Icing

3 oz. cream cheese,
    softened
2 T. half n' half
1/2 C. butter, softened
4 C. powdered sugar
1 T. lemon juice

1 tsp. vanilla
2 tsp. grated lemon peel
Pinch of salt
Yellow food coloring,
    optional

In a large bowl, combine cream cheese, half n' half and butter. Sift in powdered sugar and add lemon juice, vanilla, grated lemon peel and salt. If necessary, add more powdered sugar to thicken icing or more half n' half for a thinner consistency. If desired, mix in food coloring. Spread icing over cake. If desired, garnish with fresh apple slices.

Mountain Home Lodge
Leavenworth, Washington

Pumpkin Roll

3 eggs
1 C. sugar
2/3 C. canned pumpkin
1 tsp. lemon juice
3/4 C. flour
1 tsp. baking powder
2 tsp. cinnamon
1 tsp. ground ginger

1/2 tsp. nutmeg
1/2 tsp. salt
3/4 C. chopped walnuts
2 C. powdered sugar,
    divided
6 oz. cream cheese, softened
4 T. butter or oleo
1/2 tsp. vanilla

Preheat oven to 375°. In a large bowl, beat eggs for 5 minutes. Add sugar, canned pumpkin and lemon juice. Mix well and fold in flour, baking powder, cinnamon, ground ginger, nutmeg and salt. Spread mixture in a greased and floured 10x15" jellyroll pan. Top with chopped walnuts. Bake for 15 minutes. Sprinkle 1 cup powdered sugar over a kitchen towel. Turn baked pumpkin cake out onto towel. Carefully roll up pumpkin cake by lifting up 1 side of the towel. Roll into a log and let cool. In a separate bowl, combine remaining 1 cup powdered sugar, cream cheese, butter and vanilla. Once cool, unwrap pumpkin log and spread powdered sugar mixture evenly over cake. Rewrap pumpkin into log shape and place in refrigerator. Before serving, cut roll into slices.

Nushagak Salmon Camp Lodge
Anchorage, Alaska

Scrumptious Strawberry Coconut Cake

1 (8 oz.) pkg. cream
cheese, softened
1 1/4 C. sugar
1/2 C. plus 1/3 C.
butter, softened,
divided
2 eggs
2 tsp. vanilla
1 3/4 C. flour

1 tsp. baking powder
1/2 tsp. baking soda
1/4 tsp. salt
1/4 C. milk
1/2 C. strawberry
preserves
2 C. shredded coconut
2/3 C. brown sugar
1 tsp. cinnamon

Preheat oven to 350°. Thoroughly grease a bundt pan and set aside. In a large mixing bowl, beat cream cheese, sugar, 1/2 cup butter, eggs and vanilla at medium speed, until light and fluffy. In a separate bowl, combine flour, baking powder, baking soda and salt. Pour cream cheese mixture into dry ingredients and mix well. Pour half of the batter into prepared pan. Layer strawberry preserves over batter in pan and cover with remaining half of the batter. Bake for 40 to 45 minutes, until browned. Melt remaining 1/3 cup butter in microwave. In a separate bowl, combine melted butter, shredded coconut, brown sugar and cinnamon. Immediately top cake with coconut mixture and bake an additional 7 to 10 minutes, until topping is crunchy.

Minnewaska Lodge
Gardiner, New York

Whipped Cream
Pound Cake

1 C. butter, softened
3 C. sugar
1/2 tsp. salt
6 eggs

3 C. plus 3 tsp. cake flour
1 C. heavy whipping cream
1 tsp. vanilla or almond
   extract

Preheat oven to 300°. In a large bowl, cream together butter, sugar and salt. Beat in eggs, one at a time. Alternating, add cake flour and heavy cream. Stir in vanilla or almond extract. Pour batter into a generously greased and floured tube pan. Bake for 1 hour and 25 minutes. Let cool before serving.

Wikle Lodge
Bryson City, North Carolina

Savory Pumpkin Cake with Cream Cheese Frosting

2 C. sugar	2 tsp. baking soda
1 1/4 C. vegetable oil	1/4 tsp. salt
2 C. canned pumpkin	2 tsp. cinnamon
4 eggs	1 tsp. nutmeg
3 tsp. vanilla, divided	8 oz. cream cheese, softened
2 C. flour	1/2 C. butter, melted
1 T. baking powder	3 1/2 C. powdered sugar

Preheat oven to 350°. Grease a bundt pan and set aside. In a large bowl, combine sugar, vegetable oil, canned pumpkin, eggs and 1 teaspoon vanilla. In a separate bowl, combine flour, baking powder, baking soda, salt, cinnamon and nutmeg. Pour sugar and pumpkin mixture over dry ingredients and mix well. Pour batter into prepared pan. Bake for 35 to 40 minutes, until orange brown in color. To make frosting, in a separate bowl, combine cream cheese and melted butter, mixing until fluffy. Add powdered sugar and remaining 2 teaspoons vanilla, beating until fluffy. Let cake cool before drizzling with frosting.

Minnewaska Lodge
Gardiner, New York

Lodge Contributors

Nushagak Salmon Camp
Lodge
Anchorage, Alaska
907-522-1133

Sheep Mountain Lodge
Palmer, Alaska
877-645-5121

Lodge at Sedona –
A Luxury B&B Inn
Sedona, Arizona
800-619-4467

Pond Mountain Lodge
Eureka Springs, Arkansas
800-583-8043

Canyon Crest Lodge
Pagosa Springs, Colorado
866-532-9192

Liars' Lodge B&B
Buena Vista, Colorado
888-542-7756

Rocky Mountain Lodge
& Cabins
Cascade, Colorado
888-298-0348

Sundance Bear Lodge
Mancos, Colorado
866-529-2480

The Lodge and Spa
at Cordillera
Edwards, Colorado
800-877-3529

Mountain Top Lodge
at Dahlonega
Dahlonega, Georgia
800-526-9754

Wolf Lodge Creek B&B
Coeur d'Alene, Idaho
800-919-WOLF

Alamoosook Lodge
Orland, Maine
866-459-6393

Johnson's Allagash Lodge
Mapleton, Maine
207-764-5875

The Lodge at Moosehead Lake
Greenville, Maine
207-695-4400

Balsam Beach Resort & RV
Park
Bemidji, Minnesota
218-751-5057

Boyd Lodge
Crosslake, Minnesota
800-450-2693

Cedar Rapids Lodge
Tenstrike, Minnesota
800-233-8562

Pike Point Resort & Lodge
Tenstrike, Minnesota
800-586-2810

Prothero's Post Resort
Angle Inlet, Minnesota
888-591-7001

Three Seasons Lodge on Otter
  Tail Lake
Battle Lake, Minnesota
800-334-3679

Duck Inn
Whitefish, Montana
406-862-3825

Lake Placid Lodge
Lake Placid, New York
877-523-2700

Minnewaska Lodge
Gardiner, New York
845-255-1110

Point Au Roche Lodge
Plattsburgh, New York
518-563-8714

Snowbird Mountain Lodge
Robbinsville, North Carolina
800-941-9290

Wikle Lodge
Bryson City, North Carolina
828-488-6012

Overleaf Lodge
Yachats, Oregon
800-338-0507

Rough Creek Lodge
Glen Rose, Texas
254-965-3700

Moose Meadow Lodge
Waterbury, Vermont
802-244-5378

A B&B at Llewellyn Lodge
Lexington, Virginia
800-882-1145

Mountain Home Lodge
Leavenworth, Washington
800-414-2378

Buffalo Run Lodge
Arbovale, West Virginia
800-CALL-WVA

Evergreen Lodge
Boulder Junction, Wisconsin
715-385-2132

Lazy Cloud Lodge
Fontana, Wisconsin
262-245-5487

Ross' Teal Lake Lodge
Hayward, Wisconsin
715-462-3631

St. Germain Lodge
St. Germain, Wisconsin
715-542-3433

Boulder Lake Lodge
Pinedale, Wyoming
800-788-5401

Devils Tower Lodge
Devils Tower, Wyoming
888-314-5267

Index

Beverages, Sauces & Snacks

Breads & Sides

Main Dishes & Soups

Desserts